C-3008

M000288231

THIS IS YOUR **PASSBOOK**® FOR ...

SCALE OPERATOR

NATIONAL LEARNING CORPORATION®
passbooks.com

PASSBOOK® SERIES

THE *PASSBOOK® SERIES* has been created to prepare applicants and candidates for the ultimate academic battlefield – the examination room.

At some time in our lives, each and every one of us may be required to take an examination – for validation, matriculation, admission, qualification, registration, certification, or licensure.

Based on the assumption that every applicant or candidate has met the basic formal educational standards, has taken the required number of courses, and read the necessary texts, the *PASSBOOK® SERIES* furnishes the one special preparation which may assure passing with confidence, instead of failing with insecurity. Examination questions – together with answers – are furnished as the basic vehicle for study so that the mysteries of the examination and its compounding difficulties may be eliminated or diminished by a sure method.

This book is meant to help you pass your examination provided that you qualify and are serious in your objective.

The entire field is reviewed through the huge store of content information which is succinctly presented through a provocative and challenging approach – the question-and-answer method.

A climate of success is established by furnishing the correct answers at the end of each test.

You soon learn to recognize types of questions, forms of questions, and patterns of questioning. You may even begin to anticipate expected outcomes.

You perceive that many questions are repeated or adapted so that you can gain acute insights, which may enable you to score many sure points.

You learn how to confront new questions, or types of questions, and to attack them confidently and work out the correct answers.

You note objectives and emphases, and recognize pitfalls and dangers, so that you may make positive educational adjustments.

Moreover, you are kept fully informed in relation to new concepts, methods, practices, and directions in the field.

You discover that you arre actually taking the examination all the time: you are preparing for the examination by "taking" an examination, not by reading extraneous and/or supererogatory textbooks.

In short, this PASSBOOK®, used directedly, should be an important factor in helping you to pass your test.

SCALE OPERATOR

DUTIES

An employee in this class operates a scale to weigh vehicles at a public facility, such as highway yard, incinerator plant or refuse disposal site. The incumbent computes the weight of the contents to verify the amount of deliveries, to record the amount of materials being issued or to determine the charge for dumping refuse. Work may also involve responsibility for collecting fees, maintaining records of receipts and preparing bank deposits. Supervision is received from a supervisor responsible for the operation of the facility. Does related work as required.

SCOPE OF THE EXAMINATION

The written test will cover knowledge, skills, and/or abilities in such areas as:

1. Understanding and interpreting written material including procedures;
2. Comparing and verifying alpha and numeric characters;
3. Arithmetic reasoning; and
4. Ability to interact with the public in a courteous manner.

HOW TO TAKE A TEST

I. YOU MUST PASS AN EXAMINATION

A. *WHAT EVERY CANDIDATE SHOULD KNOW*

Examination applicants often ask us for help in preparing for the written test. What can I study in advance? What kinds of questions will be asked? How will the test be given? How will the papers be graded?

As an applicant for a civil service examination, you may be wondering about some of these things. Our purpose here is to suggest effective methods of advance study and to describe civil service examinations.

Your chances for success on this examination can be increased if you know how to prepare. Those "pre-examination jitters" can be reduced if you know what to expect. You can even experience an adventure in good citizenship if you know why civil service exams are given.

B. *WHY ARE CIVIL SERVICE EXAMINATIONS GIVEN?*

Civil service examinations are important to you in two ways. As a citizen, you want public jobs filled by employees who know how to do their work. As a job seeker, you want a fair chance to compete for that job on an equal footing with other candidates. The best-known means of accomplishing this two-fold goal is the competitive examination.

Exams are widely publicized throughout the nation. They may be administered for jobs in federal, state, city, municipal, town or village governments or agencies.

Any citizen may apply, with some limitations, such as the age or residence of applicants. Your experience and education may be reviewed to see whether you meet the requirements for the particular examination. When these requirements exist, they are reasonable and applied consistently to all applicants. Thus, a competitive examination may cause you some uneasiness now, but it is your privilege and safeguard.

C. *HOW ARE CIVIL SERVICE EXAMS DEVELOPED?*

Examinations are carefully written by trained technicians who are specialists in the field known as "psychological measurement," in consultation with recognized authorities in the field of work that the test will cover. These experts recommend the subject matter areas or skills to be tested; only those knowledges or skills important to your success on the job are included. The most reliable books and source materials available are used as references. Together, the experts and technicians judge the difficulty level of the questions.

Test technicians know how to phrase questions so that the problem is clearly stated. Their ethics do not permit "trick" or "catch" questions. Questions may have been tried out on sample groups, or subjected to statistical analysis, to determine their usefulness.

Written tests are often used in combination with performance tests, ratings of training and experience, and oral interviews. All of these measures combine to form the best-known means of finding the right person for the right job.

II. HOW TO PASS THE WRITTEN TEST

A. *NATURE OF THE EXAMINATION*

To prepare intelligently for civil service examinations, you should know how they differ from school examinations you have taken. In school you were assigned certain definite pages to read or subjects to cover. The examination questions were quite detailed and usually emphasized memory. Civil service exams, on the other hand, try to discover your present ability to perform the duties of a position, plus your potentiality to learn these duties. In other words, a civil service exam attempts to predict how successful you will be. Questions cover such a broad area that they cannot be as minute and detailed as school exam questions.

In the public service similar kinds of work, or positions, are grouped together in one "class." This process is known as *position-classification*. All the positions in a class are paid according to the salary range for that class. One class title covers all of these positions, and they are all tested by the same examination.

B. *FOUR BASIC STEPS*

1) Study the announcement

How, then, can you know what subjects to study? Our best answer is: "Learn as much as possible about the class of positions for which you've applied." The exam will test the knowledge, skills and abilities needed to do the work.

Your most valuable source of information about the position you want is the official exam announcement. This announcement lists the training and experience qualifications. Check these standards and apply only if you come reasonably close to meeting them.

The brief description of the position in the examination announcement offers some clues to the subjects which will be tested. Think about the job itself. Review the duties in your mind. Can you perform them, or are there some in which you are rusty? Fill in the blank spots in your preparation.

Many jurisdictions preview the written test in the exam announcement by including a section called "Knowledge and Abilities Required," "Scope of the Examination," or some similar heading. Here you will find out specifically what fields will be tested.

2) Review your own background

Once you learn in general what the position is all about, and what you need to know to do the work, ask yourself which subjects you already know fairly well and which need improvement. You may wonder whether to concentrate on improving your strong areas or on building some background in your fields of weakness. When the announcement has specified "some knowledge" or "considerable knowledge," or has used adjectives like "beginning principles of…" or "advanced … methods," you can get a clue as to the number and difficulty of questions to be asked in any given field. More questions, and hence broader coverage, would be included for those subjects which are more important in the work. Now weigh your strengths and weaknesses against the job requirements and prepare accordingly.

3) Determine the level of the position

Another way to tell how intensively you should prepare is to understand the level of the job for which you are applying. Is it the entering level? In other words, is this the position in which beginners in a field of work are hired? Or is it an intermediate or advanced level? Sometimes this is indicated by such words as "Junior" or "Senior" in the class title. Other jurisdictions use Roman numerals to designate the level – Clerk I, Clerk II, for example. The word "Supervisor" sometimes appears in the title. If the level is not indicated by the title, check the description of duties. Will you be working under very close supervision, or will you have responsibility for independent decisions in this work?

4) Choose appropriate study materials

Now that you know the subjects to be examined and the relative amount of each subject to be covered, you can choose suitable study materials. For beginning level jobs, or even advanced ones, if you have a pronounced weakness in some aspect of your training, read a modern, standard textbook in that field. Be sure it is up to date and has general coverage. Such books are normally available at your library, and the librarian will be glad to help you locate one. For entry-level positions, questions of appropriate difficulty are chosen – neither highly advanced questions, nor those too simple. Such questions require careful thought but not advanced training.

If the position for which you are applying is technical or advanced, you will read more advanced, specialized material. If you are already familiar with the basic principles of your field, elementary textbooks would waste your time. Concentrate on advanced textbooks and technical periodicals. Think through the concepts and review difficult problems in your field.

These are all general sources. You can get more ideas on your own initiative, following these leads. For example, training manuals and publications of the government agency which employs workers in your field can be useful, particularly for technical and professional positions. A letter or visit to the government department involved may result in more specific study suggestions, and certainly will provide you with a more definite idea of the exact nature of the position you are seeking.

III. KINDS OF TESTS

Tests are used for purposes other than measuring knowledge and ability to perform specified duties. For some positions, it is equally important to test ability to make adjustments to new situations or to profit from training. In others, basic mental abilities not dependent on information are essential. Questions which test these things may not appear as pertinent to the duties of the position as those which test for knowledge and information. Yet they are often highly important parts of a fair examination. For very general questions, it is almost impossible to help you direct your study efforts. What we can do is to point out some of the more common of these general abilities needed in public service positions and describe some typical questions.

1) General information

Broad, general information has been found useful for predicting job success in some kinds of work. This is tested in a variety of ways, from vocabulary lists to questions about current events. Basic background in some field of work, such as sociology or economics, may be sampled in a group of questions. Often these are principles which have become familiar to most persons through exposure rather than through formal training. It is difficult to advise you how to study for these questions; being alert to the world around you is our best suggestion.

2) Verbal ability

An example of an ability needed in many positions is verbal or language ability. Verbal ability is, in brief, the ability to use and understand words. Vocabulary and grammar tests are typical measures of this ability. Reading comprehension or paragraph interpretation questions are common in many kinds of civil service tests. You are given a paragraph of written material and asked to find its central meaning.

3) Numerical ability

Number skills can be tested by the familiar arithmetic problem, by checking paired lists of numbers to see which are alike and which are different, or by interpreting charts and graphs. In the latter test, a graph may be printed in the test booklet which you are asked to use as the basis for answering questions.

4) Observation

A popular test for law-enforcement positions is the observation test. A picture is shown to you for several minutes, then taken away. Questions about the picture test your ability to observe both details and larger elements.

5) Following directions

In many positions in the public service, the employee must be able to carry out written instructions dependably and accurately. You may be given a chart with several columns, each column listing a variety of information. The questions require you to carry out directions involving the information given in the chart.

6) Skills and aptitudes

Performance tests effectively measure some manual skills and aptitudes. When the skill is one in which you are trained, such as typing or shorthand, you can practice. These tests are often very much like those given in business school or high school courses. For many of the other skills and aptitudes, however, no short-time preparation can be made. Skills and abilities natural to you or that you have developed throughout your lifetime are being tested.

Many of the general questions just described provide all the data needed to answer the questions and ask you to use your reasoning ability to find the answers. Your best preparation for these tests, as well as for tests of facts and ideas, is to be at your physical and mental best. You, no doubt, have your own methods of getting into an exam-taking mood and keeping "in shape." The next section lists some ideas on this subject.

IV. KINDS OF QUESTIONS

Only rarely is the "essay" question, which you answer in narrative form, used in civil service tests. Civil service tests are usually of the short-answer type. Full instructions for answering these questions will be given to you at the examination. But in case this is your first experience with short-answer questions and separate answer sheets, here is what you need to know:

1) Multiple-choice Questions

Most popular of the short-answer questions is the "multiple choice" or "best answer" question. It can be used, for example, to test for factual knowledge, ability to solve problems or judgment in meeting situations found at work.

A multiple-choice question is normally one of three types—

- It can begin with an incomplete statement followed by several possible endings. You are to find the one ending which *best* completes the statement, although some of the others may not be entirely wrong.
- It can also be a complete statement in the form of a question which is answered by choosing one of the statements listed.
- It can be in the form of a problem – again you select the best answer.

Here is an example of a multiple-choice question with a discussion which should give you some clues as to the method for choosing the right answer:

When an employee has a complaint about his assignment, the action which will *best* help him overcome his difficulty is to
   A. discuss his difficulty with his coworkers
   B. take the problem to the head of the organization
   C. take the problem to the person who gave him the assignment
   D. say nothing to anyone about his complaint

In answering this question, you should study each of the choices to find which is best. Consider choice "A" – Certainly an employee may discuss his complaint with fellow employees, but no change or improvement can result, and the complaint remains unresolved. Choice "B" is a poor choice since the head of the organization probably does not know what assignment you have been given, and taking your problem to him is known as "going over the head" of the supervisor. The supervisor, or person who made the assignment, is the person who can clarify it or correct any injustice. Choice "C" is, therefore, correct. To say nothing, as in choice "D," is unwise. Supervisors have and interest in knowing the problems employees are facing, and the employee is seeking a solution to his problem.

2) True/False Questions

The "true/false" or "right/wrong" form of question is sometimes used. Here a complete statement is given. Your job is to decide whether the statement is right or wrong.

SAMPLE: A roaming cell-phone call to a nearby city costs less than a non-roaming call to a distant city.

This statement is wrong, or false, since roaming calls are more expensive.
This is not a complete list of all possible question forms, although most of the others are variations of these common types. You will always get complete directions for

answering questions. Be sure you understand *how* to mark your answers – ask questions until you do.

V. RECORDING YOUR ANSWERS

Computer terminals are used more and more today for many different kinds of exams.

For an examination with very few applicants, you may be told to record your answers in the test booklet itself. Separate answer sheets are much more common. If this separate answer sheet is to be scored by machine – and this is often the case – it is highly important that you mark your answers correctly in order to get credit.

An electronic scoring machine is often used in civil service offices because of the speed with which papers can be scored. Machine-scored answer sheets must be marked with a pencil, which will be given to you. This pencil has a high graphite content which responds to the electronic scoring machine. As a matter of fact, stray dots may register as answers, so do not let your pencil rest on the answer sheet while you are pondering the correct answer. Also, if your pencil lead breaks or is otherwise defective, ask for another.

Since the answer sheet will be dropped in a slot in the scoring machine, be careful not to bend the corners or get the paper crumpled.

The answer sheet normally has five vertical columns of numbers, with 30 numbers to a column. These numbers correspond to the question numbers in your test booklet. After each number, going across the page are four or five pairs of dotted lines. These short dotted lines have small letters or numbers above them. The first two pairs may also have a "T" or "F" above the letters. This indicates that the first two pairs only are to be used if the questions are of the true-false type. If the questions are multiple choice, disregard the "T" and "F" and pay attention only to the small letters or numbers.

Answer your questions in the manner of the sample that follows:

32. The largest city in the United States is
    A. Washington, D.C.
    B. New York City
    C. Chicago
    D. Detroit
    E. San Francisco

1) Choose the answer you think is best. (New York City is the largest, so "B" is correct.)
2) Find the row of dotted lines numbered the same as the question you are answering. (Find row number 32)
3) Find the pair of dotted lines corresponding to the answer. (Find the pair of lines under the mark "B.")
4) Make a solid black mark between the dotted lines.

VI. BEFORE THE TEST

Common sense will help you find procedures to follow to get ready for an examination. Too many of us, however, overlook these sensible measures. Indeed, nervousness and fatigue have been found to be the most serious reasons why applicants fail to do their best on civil service tests. Here is a list of reminders:

- Begin your preparation early – Don't wait until the last minute to go scurrying around for books and materials or to find out what the position is all about.
- Prepare continuously – An hour a night for a week is better than an all-night cram session. This has been definitely established. What is more, a night a week for a month will return better dividends than crowding your study into a shorter period of time.
- Locate the place of the exam – You have been sent a notice telling you when and where to report for the examination. If the location is in a different town or otherwise unfamiliar to you, it would be well to inquire the best route and learn something about the building.
- Relax the night before the test – Allow your mind to rest. Do not study at all that night. Plan some mild recreation or diversion; then go to bed early and get a good night's sleep.
- Get up early enough to make a leisurely trip to the place for the test – This way unforeseen events, traffic snarls, unfamiliar buildings, etc. will not upset you.
- Dress comfortably – A written test is not a fashion show. You will be known by number and not by name, so wear something comfortable.
- Leave excess paraphernalia at home – Shopping bags and odd bundles will get in your way. You need bring only the items mentioned in the official notice you received; usually everything you need is provided. Do not bring reference books to the exam. They will only confuse those last minutes and be taken away from you when in the test room.
- Arrive somewhat ahead of time – If because of transportation schedules you must get there very early, bring a newspaper or magazine to take your mind off yourself while waiting.
- Locate the examination room – When you have found the proper room, you will be directed to the seat or part of the room where you will sit. Sometimes you are given a sheet of instructions to read while you are waiting. Do not fill out any forms until you are told to do so; just read them and be prepared.
- Relax and prepare to listen to the instructions
- If you have any physical problem that may keep you from doing your best, be sure to tell the test administrator. If you are sick or in poor health, you really cannot do your best on the exam. You can come back and take the test some other time.

VII. AT THE TEST

The day of the test is here and you have the test booklet in your hand. The temptation to get going is very strong. Caution! There is more to success than knowing the right answers. You must know how to identify your papers and understand variations in the type of short-answer question used in this particular examination. Follow these suggestions for maximum results from your efforts:

1) Cooperate with the monitor

The test administrator has a duty to create a situation in which you can be as much at ease as possible. He will give instructions, tell you when to begin, check to see that you are marking your answer sheet correctly, and so on. He is not there to guard you, although he will see that your competitors do not take unfair advantage. He wants to help you do your best.

2) Listen to all instructions

Don't jump the gun! Wait until you understand all directions. In most civil service tests you get more time than you need to answer the questions. So don't be in a hurry. Read each word of instructions until you clearly understand the meaning. Study the examples, listen to all announcements and follow directions. Ask questions if you do not understand what to do.

3) Identify your papers

Civil service exams are usually identified by number only. You will be assigned a number; you must not put your name on your test papers. Be sure to copy your number correctly. Since more than one exam may be given, copy your exact examination title.

4) Plan your time

Unless you are told that a test is a "speed" or "rate of work" test, speed itself is usually not important. Time enough to answer all the questions will be provided, but this does not mean that you have all day. An overall time limit has been set. Divide the total time (in minutes) by the number of questions to determine the approximate time you have for each question.

5) Do not linger over difficult questions

If you come across a difficult question, mark it with a paper clip (useful to have along) and come back to it when you have been through the booklet. One caution if you do this – be sure to skip a number on your answer sheet as well. Check often to be sure that you have not lost your place and that you are marking in the row numbered the same as the question you are answering.

6) Read the questions

Be sure you know what the question asks! Many capable people are unsuccessful because they failed to *read* the questions correctly.

7) Answer all questions

Unless you have been instructed that a penalty will be deducted for incorrect answers, it is better to guess than to omit a question.

8) Speed tests

It is often better NOT to guess on speed tests. It has been found that on timed tests people are tempted to spend the last few seconds before time is called in marking answers at random – without even reading them – in the hope of picking up a few extra points. To discourage this practice, the instructions may warn you that your score will be "corrected" for guessing. That is, a penalty will be applied. The incorrect answers will be deducted from the correct ones, or some other penalty formula will be used.

9) Review your answers

If you finish before time is called, go back to the questions you guessed or omitted to give them further thought. Review other answers if you have time.

10) Return your test materials

If you are ready to leave before others have finished or time is called, take ALL your materials to the monitor and leave quietly. Never take any test material with you. The monitor can discover whose papers are not complete, and taking a test booklet may be grounds for disqualification.

VIII. EXAMINATION TECHNIQUES

1) Read the general instructions carefully. These are usually printed on the first page of the exam booklet. As a rule, these instructions refer to the timing of the examination; the fact that you should not start work until the signal and must stop work at a signal, etc. If there are any *special* instructions, such as a choice of questions to be answered, make sure that you note this instruction carefully.

2) When you are ready to start work on the examination, that is as soon as the signal has been given, read the instructions to each question booklet, underline any key words or phrases, such as *least, best, outline, describe* and the like. In this way you will tend to answer as requested rather than discover on reviewing your paper that you *listed without describing*, that you selected the *worst* choice rather than the *best* choice, etc.

3) If the examination is of the objective or multiple-choice type – that is, each question will also give a series of possible answers: A, B, C or D, and you are called upon to select the best answer and write the letter next to that answer on your answer paper – it is advisable to start answering each question in turn. There may be anywhere from 50 to 100 such questions in the three or four hours allotted and you can see how much time would be taken if you read through all the questions before beginning to answer any. Furthermore, if you come across a question or group of questions which you know would be difficult to answer, it would undoubtedly affect your handling of all the other questions.

4) If the examination is of the essay type and contains but a few questions, it is a moot point as to whether you should read all the questions before starting to answer any one. Of course, if you are given a choice – say five out of seven and the like – then it is essential to read all the questions so you can eliminate the two that are most difficult. If, however, you are asked to answer all the questions, there may be danger in trying to answer the easiest one first because you may find that you will spend too much time on it. The best technique is to answer the first question, then proceed to the second, etc.

5) Time your answers. Before the exam begins, write down the time it started, then add the time allowed for the examination and write down the time it must be completed, then divide the time available somewhat as follows:

- If 3-1/2 hours are allowed, that would be 210 minutes. If you have 80 objective-type questions, that would be an average of 2-1/2 minutes per question. Allow yourself no more than 2 minutes per question, or a total of 160 minutes, which will permit about 50 minutes to review.
- If for the time allotment of 210 minutes there are 7 essay questions to answer, that would average about 30 minutes a question. Give yourself only 25 minutes per question so that you have about 35 minutes to review.

6) The most important instruction is to *read each question* and make sure you know what is wanted. The second most important instruction is to *time yourself properly* so that you answer every question. The third most important instruction is to *answer every question*. Guess if you have to but include something for each question. Remember that you will receive no credit for a blank and will probably receive some credit if you write something in answer to an essay question. If you guess a letter – say "B" for a multiple-choice question – you may have guessed right. If you leave a blank as an answer to a multiple-choice question, the examiners may respect your feelings but it will not add a point to your score. Some exams may penalize you for wrong answers, so in such cases *only*, you may not want to guess unless you have some basis for your answer.

7) Suggestions
    a. Objective-type questions
        1. Examine the question booklet for proper sequence of pages and questions
        2. Read all instructions carefully
        3. Skip any question which seems too difficult; return to it after all other questions have been answered
        4. Apportion your time properly; do not spend too much time on any single question or group of questions
        5. Note and underline key words – *all, most, fewest, least, best, worst, same, opposite,* etc.
        6. Pay particular attention to negatives
        7. Note unusual option, e.g., unduly long, short, complex, different or similar in content to the body of the question
        8. Observe the use of "hedging" words – *probably, may, most likely,* etc.
        9. Make sure that your answer is put next to the same number as the question
        10. Do not second-guess unless you have good reason to believe the second answer is definitely more correct
        11. Cross out original answer if you decide another answer is more accurate; do not erase until you are ready to hand your paper in
        12. Answer all questions; guess unless instructed otherwise
        13. Leave time for review

    b. Essay questions
        1. Read each question carefully
        2. Determine exactly what is wanted. Underline key words or phrases.
        3. Decide on outline or paragraph answer

4. Include many different points and elements unless asked to develop any one or two points or elements
5. Show impartiality by giving pros and cons unless directed to select one side only
6. Make and write down any assumptions you find necessary to answer the questions
7. Watch your English, grammar, punctuation and choice of words
8. Time your answers; don't crowd material

8) Answering the essay question

Most essay questions can be answered by framing the specific response around several key words or ideas. Here are a few such key words or ideas:

M's: manpower, materials, methods, money, management
P's: purpose, program, policy, plan, procedure, practice, problems, pitfalls, personnel, public relations
   a. Six basic steps in handling problems:
       1. Preliminary plan and background development
       2. Collect information, data and facts
       3. Analyze and interpret information, data and facts
       4. Analyze and develop solutions as well as make recommendations
       5. Prepare report and sell recommendations
       6. Install recommendations and follow up effectiveness

   b. Pitfalls to avoid
       1. *Taking things for granted* – A statement of the situation does not necessarily imply that each of the elements is necessarily true; for example, a complaint may be invalid and biased so that all that can be taken for granted is that a complaint has been registered
       2. *Considering only one side of a situation* – Wherever possible, indicate several alternatives and then point out the reasons you selected the best one
       3. *Failing to indicate follow up* – Whenever your answer indicates action on your part, make certain that you will take proper follow-up action to see how successful your recommendations, procedures or actions turn out to be
       4. *Taking too long in answering any single question* – Remember to time your answers properly

IX. AFTER THE TEST

Scoring procedures differ in detail among civil service jurisdictions although the general principles are the same. Whether the papers are hand-scored or graded by machine we have described, they are nearly always graded by number. That is, the person who marks the paper knows only the number – never the name – of the applicant. Not until all the papers have been graded will they be matched with names. If other tests, such as training and experience or oral interview ratings have been given, scores will be combined. Different parts of the examination usually have different weights. For example, the written test might count 60 percent of the final grade, and a rating of training and experience 40 percent. In many jurisdictions, veterans will have a certain number of points added to their grades.

After the final grade has been determined, the names are placed in grade order and an eligible list is established. There are various methods for resolving ties between those who get the same final grade – probably the most common is to place first the name of the person whose application was received first. Job offers are made from the eligible list in the order the names appear on it. You will be notified of your grade and your rank as soon as all these computations have been made. This will be done as rapidly as possible.

People who are found to meet the requirements in the announcement are called "eligibles." Their names are put on a list of eligible candidates. An eligible's chances of getting a job depend on how high he stands on this list and how fast agencies are filling jobs from the list.

When a job is to be filled from a list of eligibles, the agency asks for the names of people on the list of eligibles for that job. When the civil service commission receives this request, it sends to the agency the names of the three people highest on this list. Or, if the job to be filled has specialized requirements, the office sends the agency the names of the top three persons who meet these requirements from the general list.

The appointing officer makes a choice from among the three people whose names were sent to him. If the selected person accepts the appointment, the names of the others are put back on the list to be considered for future openings.

That is the rule in hiring from all kinds of eligible lists, whether they are for typist, carpenter, chemist, or something else. For every vacancy, the appointing officer has his choice of any one of the top three eligibles on the list. This explains why the person whose name is on top of the list sometimes does not get an appointment when some of the persons lower on the list do. If the appointing officer chooses the second or third eligible, the No. 1 eligible does not get a job at once, but stays on the list until he is appointed or the list is terminated.

X. HOW TO PASS THE INTERVIEW TEST

The examination for which you applied requires an oral interview test. You have already taken the written test and you are now being called for the interview test – the final part of the formal examination.

You may think that it is not possible to prepare for an interview test and that there are no procedures to follow during an interview. Our purpose is to point out some things you can do in advance that will help you and some good rules to follow and pitfalls to avoid while you are being interviewed.

What is an interview supposed to test?
The written examination is designed to test the technical knowledge and competence of the candidate; the oral is designed to evaluate intangible qualities, not readily measured otherwise, and to establish a list showing the relative fitness of each candidate – as measured against his competitors – for the position sought. Scoring is not on the basis of "right" and "wrong," but on a sliding scale of values ranging from "not passable" to "outstanding." As a matter of fact, it is possible to achieve a relatively low score without a single "incorrect" answer because of evident weakness in the qualities being measured.

Occasionally, an examination may consist entirely of an oral test – either an individual or a group oral. In such cases, information is sought concerning the technical knowledges and abilities of the candidate, since there has been no written examination for this purpose. More commonly, however, an oral test is used to supplement a written examination.

Who conducts interviews?

The composition of oral boards varies among different jurisdictions. In nearly all, a representative of the personnel department serves as chairman. One of the members of the board may be a representative of the department in which the candidate would work. In some cases, "outside experts" are used, and, frequently, a businessman or some other representative of the general public is asked to serve. Labor and management or other special groups may be represented. The aim is to secure the services of experts in the appropriate field.

However the board is composed, it is a good idea (and not at all improper or unethical) to ascertain in advance of the interview who the members are and what groups they represent. When you are introduced to them, you will have some idea of their backgrounds and interests, and at least you will not stutter and stammer over their names.

What should be done before the interview?

While knowledge about the board members is useful and takes some of the surprise element out of the interview, there is other preparation which is more substantive. It *is* possible to prepare for an oral interview – in several ways:

1) Keep a copy of your application and review it carefully before the interview

This may be the only document before the oral board, and the starting point of the interview. Know what education and experience you have listed there, and the sequence and dates of all of it. Sometimes the board will ask you to review the highlights of your experience for them; you should not have to hem and haw doing it.

2) Study the class specification and the examination announcement

Usually, the oral board has one or both of these to guide them. The qualities, characteristics or knowledges required by the position sought are stated in these documents. They offer valuable clues as to the nature of the oral interview. For example, if the job involves supervisory responsibilities, the announcement will usually indicate that knowledge of modern supervisory methods and the qualifications of the candidate as a supervisor will be tested. If so, you can expect such questions, frequently in the form of a hypothetical situation which you are expected to solve. NEVER go into an oral without knowledge of the duties and responsibilities of the job you seek.

3) Think through each qualification required

Try to visualize the kind of questions you would ask if you were a board member. How well could you answer them? Try especially to appraise your own knowledge and background in each area, *measured against the job sought*, and identify any areas in which you are weak. Be critical and realistic – do not flatter yourself.

4) Do some general reading in areas in which you feel you may be weak

For example, if the job involves supervision and your past experience has NOT, some general reading in supervisory methods and practices, particularly in the field of human relations, might be useful. Do NOT study agency procedures or detailed manuals. The oral board will be testing your understanding and capacity, not your memory.

5) Get a good night's sleep and watch your general health and mental attitude

You will want a clear head at the interview. Take care of a cold or any other minor ailment, and of course, no hangovers.

What should be done on the day of the interview?

Now comes the day of the interview itself. Give yourself plenty of time to get there. Plan to arrive somewhat ahead of the scheduled time, particularly if your appointment is in the fore part of the day. If a previous candidate fails to appear, the board might be ready for you a bit early. By early afternoon an oral board is almost invariably behind schedule if there are many candidates, and you may have to wait. Take along a book or magazine to read, or your application to review, but leave any extraneous material in the waiting room when you go in for your interview. In any event, relax and compose yourself.

The matter of dress is important. The board is forming impressions about you – from your experience, your manners, your attitude, and your appearance. Give your personal appearance careful attention. Dress your best, but not your flashiest. Choose conservative, appropriate clothing, and be sure it is immaculate. This is a business interview, and your appearance should indicate that you regard it as such. Besides, being well groomed and properly dressed will help boost your confidence.

Sooner or later, someone will call your name and escort you into the interview room. *This is it.* From here on you are on your own. It is too late for any more preparation. But remember, you asked for this opportunity to prove your fitness, and you are here because your request was granted.

What happens when you go in?

The usual sequence of events will be as follows: The clerk (who is often the board stenographer) will introduce you to the chairman of the oral board, who will introduce you to the other members of the board. Acknowledge the introductions before you sit down. Do not be surprised if you find a microphone facing you or a stenotypist sitting by. Oral interviews are usually recorded in the event of an appeal or other review.

Usually the chairman of the board will open the interview by reviewing the highlights of your education and work experience from your application – primarily for the benefit of the other members of the board, as well as to get the material into the record. Do not interrupt or comment unless there is an error or significant misinterpretation; if that is the case, do not hesitate. But do not quibble about insignificant matters. Also, he will usually ask you some question about your education, experience or your present job – partly to get you to start talking and to establish the interviewing "rapport." He may start the actual questioning, or turn it over to one of the other members. Frequently, each member undertakes the questioning on a particular area, one in which he is perhaps most competent, so you can expect each member to participate in the examination. Because time is limited, you may also expect some rather abrupt switches in the direction the questioning takes, so do not be upset by it. Normally, a board member will not pursue a single line of questioning unless he discovers a particular strength or weakness.

After each member has participated, the chairman will usually ask whether any member has any further questions, then will ask you if you have anything you wish to add. Unless you are expecting this question, it may floor you. Worse, it may start you off on an extended, extemporaneous speech. The board is not usually seeking more information. The question is principally to offer you a last opportunity to present further qualifications or to indicate that you have nothing to add. So, if you feel that a significant qualification or characteristic has been overlooked, it is proper to point it out in a sentence or so. Do not compliment the board on the thoroughness of their examination – they have been sketchy, and you know it. If you wish, merely say, "No thank you, I have nothing further to add." This is a point where you can "talk yourself out" of a good impression or fail to present an important bit of information. Remember, *you close the interview yourself.*

The chairman will then say, "That is all, Mr. _____, thank you." Do not be startled; the interview is over, and quicker than you think. Thank him, gather your belongings and take your leave. Save your sigh of relief for the other side of the door.

How to put your best foot forward
Throughout this entire process, you may feel that the board individually and collectively is trying to pierce your defenses, seek out your hidden weaknesses and embarrass and confuse you. Actually, this is not true. They are obliged to make an appraisal of your qualifications for the job you are seeking, and they want to see you in your best light. Remember, they must interview all candidates and a non-cooperative candidate may become a failure in spite of their best efforts to bring out his qualifications. Here are 15 suggestions that will help you:

1) Be natural – Keep your attitude confident, not cocky
If you are not confident that you can do the job, do not expect the board to be. Do not apologize for your weaknesses, try to bring out your strong points. The board is interested in a positive, not negative, presentation. Cockiness will antagonize any board member and make him wonder if you are covering up a weakness by a false show of strength.

2) Get comfortable, but don't lounge or sprawl
Sit erectly but not stiffly. A careless posture may lead the board to conclude that you are careless in other things, or at least that you are not impressed by the importance of the occasion. Either conclusion is natural, even if incorrect. Do not fuss with your clothing, a pencil or an ashtray. Your hands may occasionally be useful to emphasize a point; do not let them become a point of distraction.

3) Do not wisecrack or make small talk
This is a serious situation, and your attitude should show that you consider it as such. Further, the time of the board is limited – they do not want to waste it, and neither should you.

4) Do not exaggerate your experience or abilities
In the first place, from information in the application or other interviews and sources, the board may know more about you than you think. Secondly, you probably will not get away with it. An experienced board is rather adept at spotting such a situation, so do not take the chance.

5) If you know a board member, do not make a point of it, yet do not hide it

Certainly you are not fooling him, and probably not the other members of the board. Do not try to take advantage of your acquaintanceship – it will probably do you little good.

6) Do not dominate the interview

Let the board do that. They will give you the clues – do not assume that you have to do all the talking. Realize that the board has a number of questions to ask you, and do not try to take up all the interview time by showing off your extensive knowledge of the answer to the first one.

7) Be attentive

You only have 20 minutes or so, and you should keep your attention at its sharpest throughout. When a member is addressing a problem or question to you, give him your undivided attention. Address your reply principally to him, but do not exclude the other board members.

8) Do not interrupt

A board member may be stating a problem for you to analyze. He will ask you a question when the time comes. Let him state the problem, and wait for the question.

9) Make sure you understand the question

Do not try to answer until you are sure what the question is. If it is not clear, restate it in your own words or ask the board member to clarify it for you. However, do not haggle about minor elements.

10) Reply promptly but not hastily

A common entry on oral board rating sheets is "candidate responded readily," or "candidate hesitated in replies." Respond as promptly and quickly as you can, but do not jump to a hasty, ill-considered answer.

11) Do not be peremptory in your answers

A brief answer is proper – but do not fire your answer back. That is a losing game from your point of view. The board member can probably ask questions much faster than you can answer them.

12) Do not try to create the answer you think the board member wants

He is interested in what kind of mind you have and how it works – not in playing games. Furthermore, he can usually spot this practice and will actually grade you down on it.

13) Do not switch sides in your reply merely to agree with a board member

Frequently, a member will take a contrary position merely to draw you out and to see if you are willing and able to defend your point of view. Do not start a debate, yet do not surrender a good position. If a position is worth taking, it is worth defending.

14) Do not be afraid to admit an error in judgment if you are shown to be wrong

The board knows that you are forced to reply without any opportunity for careful consideration. Your answer may be demonstrably wrong. If so, admit it and get on with the interview.

15) Do not dwell at length on your present job

The opening question may relate to your present assignment. Answer the question but do not go into an extended discussion. You are being examined for a *new* job, not your present one. As a matter of fact, try to phrase ALL your answers in terms of the job for which you are being examined.

Basis of Rating

Probably you will forget most of these "do's" and "don'ts" when you walk into the oral interview room. Even remembering them all will not ensure you a passing grade. Perhaps you did not have the qualifications in the first place. But remembering them will help you to put your best foot forward, without treading on the toes of the board members.

Rumor and popular opinion to the contrary notwithstanding, an oral board wants you to make the best appearance possible. They know you are under pressure – but they also want to see how you respond to it as a guide to what your reaction would be under the pressures of the job you seek. They will be influenced by the degree of poise you display, the personal traits you show and the manner in which you respond.

ABOUT THIS BOOK

This book contains tests divided into Examination Sections. Go through each test, answering every question in the margin. At the end of each test look at the answer key and check your answers. On the ones you got wrong, look at the right answer choice and learn. Do not fill in the answers first. Do not memorize the questions and answers, but understand the answer and principles involved. On your test, the questions will likely be different from the samples. Questions are changed and new ones added. If you understand these past questions you should have success with any changes that arise. Tests may consist of several types of questions. We have additional books on each subject should more study be advisable or necessary for you. Finally, the more you study, the better prepared you will be. This book is intended to be the last thing you study before you walk into the examination room. Prior study of relevant texts is also recommended. NLC publishes some of these in our Fundamental Series. Knowledge and good sense are important factors in passing your exam. Good luck also helps. So now study this Passbook, absorb the material contained within and take that knowledge into the examination. Then do your best to pass that exam.

––––––––

EXAMINATION SECTION

EXAMINATION SECTION
TEST 1

DIRECTIONS: Each question or incomplete statement is followed by several suggested answers or completions. Select the one that BEST answers the question or completes the statement. *PRINT THE LETTER OF THE CORRECT ANSWER IN THE SPACE AT THE RIGHT.*

NOTE: In balanced levers, as used in weighing devices, the basic principle is that the product of the force or weight acting on one arm multiplied by the distance of that force from the center of rotation must be equal to the product of the force or weight acting on the other arm multiplied by its distance from the center of rotation.

Questions 1-3.

DIRECTIONS: Questions 1 through 3, inclusive, are to be answered on the basis of the diagrams of balanced levers shown below. P is the center of rotation, W is the weight on the lever, F is the balancing force.

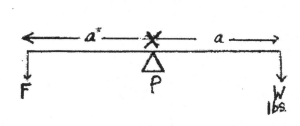 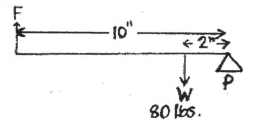

1. In Diagram 1, the force F required to balance the weight W lbs. on the lever shown is equal to _____ lbs.   1.____

    A. a/W   B. W/a   C. W   D. Wa

2. In Diagram 2, the force F required to balance the weight of 80 lbs. on the lever shown is _____ lbs.   2.____

    A. 4   B. 8   C. 16   D. 32

3. The mechanical advantage of the lever shown in Diagram 2 is   3.____

    A. 4   B. 5   C. 8   D. 12

4. Of the following, the MOST important reason for making counterpoise weights of hard durable metal is that   4.____

    A. the markings on the weights can be more easily read
    B. their weights are not likely to change much with use and there is greater accuracy in weighing operations
    C. they can be more easily tested by an inspector
    D. they can more easily be made to conform to permitted tolerances

1

5. A platform scale in good working order is so constructed that a 1-lb. weight can balance 50 lbs. placed on the platform.
   If a load of 48 lbs. is placed on the platform and the scale balances when the alleged 1 lb. weight is used, then the actual weight of the balancing weight is MOST NEARLY. _____ lbs.

   A. .920   B. .960   C. 1.04   D. 1.06

6. The PRINCIPAL reason for the establishment of tolerances in the use of weighing and measuring devices is that

   A. it is extremely difficult to construct devices which will weigh or measure with absolute accuracy
   B. it saves time in carrying on weighing or measuring operations
   C. it simplifies the work of inspectors of weights and measures
   D. there are so many different types of weighing and measuring devices in use

7. The use of the simple straight face spring scale depends upon the principle that the stretch of the spring is

   A. dependent upon the material of which the weight acting on it is made
   B. different for identical weights acting on it
   C. directly proportional to the weight acting on it
   D. inversely proportional to the weight acting on it

8. Suppose that, in the part of a computing scale which shows the cost of the goods purchased, the indicating chart is divided into as many equal spaces per pound as the price per pound.
   If the price is 32 cents a pound and the indicator is at the end of the 8th space, the weight of the goods purchased is _____ ounces.

   A. 2   B. 4   C. 6   D. 8

9. The multiplication factor of a given scale is 33 1/3 to 1. If the load on the scale is 100 pounds, the weight required to counterbalance it is _____ pound(s).

   A. 1/3   B. 2/3   C. 3   D. 3 1/3

10. Of the following, the MOST likely reason why the metric system has NOT been widely adopted in the United States is that

    A. custom and long usage of other systems tend to prevent change to the metric system
    B. systems used in the United States are fixed by law
    C. the metric system is difficult to use in making ordinary calculations connected with weights and measures
    D. the metric system is useful in scientific work only

11. The Apothecaries' Weight system is MOST likely to be used by

    A. engineers   B. jewelers
    C. pharmacists   D. physicists

12. The number of bushels in 128 pecks is 12.____

    A. 8   B. 32   C. 64   D. 256

13. The abbreviation *kw* stands for a unit used to measure 13.____

    A. cylindrical volume   B. distance
    C. electric current   D. power

14. If four rings each weigh 20 pennyweights, the one likely to contain the MOST gold is the one marked _____ karat. 14.____

    A. 10   B. 12   C. 14   D. 24

15. The LEAST accurate of the following statements is: 15.____

    A. Eight gills equals one pint
    B. One rod equals 5.5 yards
    C. The dram is used as a unit in both Apothecaries' Fluid Measure and Apothecaries' Weight
    D. The kilometer is equal to 1000 meters

16. The one of the following which is of MOST importance to a consumer of packaged goods is the 16.____

    A. gross weight   B. net weight
    C. package size   D. tare weight

17. The quality grades for canned fruits and vegetables are established by the 17.____

    A. Association of Official Agricultural Chemists
    B. National Bureau of Statistics
    C. City Health Code
    D. U.S. Department of Agriculture

18. The number of Fahrenheit degrees between the freezing point and boiling point of water is 18.____

    A. 32   B. 64   C. 100   D. 180

19. A micrometer is an instrument ordinarily used to measure very small 19.____

    A. densities   B. thicknesses
    C. volumes   D. weights

20. The drained weight of a can of vegetables refers to the weight of the 20.____

    A. contents after the liquid is poured off
    B. dry empty can
    C. liquid poured off
    D. wet empty can

21. Of the following, the one which is NOT considered kosher food during the Passover sea-   21.____
son is

    A. eggs
    B. fermented cereal products
    C. spices
    D. the forequarters of properly slaughtered lamb

22. The symbol B.T.U. stands for a unit of   22.____

    A. electricity   B. heat
    C. temperature   D. D, volume

23. The one of the following which is likely to be LEAST accurate when used as a measure   23.____
of length is

    A. a tape made of steel
    B. a wooden yardstick with metal ends
    C. a yardstick covered with metal
    D. the distance between upholstery tacks driven into a store counter

24. The method used by an official grader to indicate the grade of a wholesale cut of beef is   24.____
to

    A. place a cardboard tag bearing the grade name on the cut of beef
    B. place a metal tag bearing the grade name on the cut of beef
    C. stamp the grade name directly on the cut of beef
    D. use a harmless paste to attach a certificate bearing the grade name directly on the
       cut of beef

25. Of the following, the MOST accurate statement about the metric system is that   25.____

    A. it has no standards for dry measure
    B. it is a decimal system
    C. its units are based upon the number 12
    D. one kilometer in the metric system is approximately equal to one mile

KEY (CORRECT ANSWERS)

1.	C		11.	C
2.	C		12.	B
3.	B		13.	D
4.	B		14.	D
5.	B		15.	A
6.	A		16.	B
7.	C		17.	D
8.	B		18.	D
9.	C		19.	B
10.	A		20.	A

21.	B
22.	B
23.	D
24.	C
25.	B

TEST 2

DIRECTIONS: Each question or incomplete statement is followed by several suggested answers or completions. Select the one that BEST answers the question or completes the statement. *PRINT THE LETTER OF THE CORRECT ANSWER IN THE SPACE AT THE RIGHT.*

1. The *cord,* the unit by which wood cut for fuel is commonly sold, is a unit of   1._____

    A.   area   B.   length   C.   volume   D.   weight

2. A thermostat is an instrument or device which functions as a result of changes in   2._____

    A.   electric current
    B.   speed of flow of a liquid
    C.   speed of travel of a vehicle
    D.   temperature

3. Coke is a type of   3._____

    A.   liquid fuel additive
    B.   liquid fuel derived from petroleum
    C.   solid fuel derived from coal
    D.   wood used for fuel

4. The abbreviation *ml* stands for   4._____

    A.   mile   B.   milliliter
    C.   millimeter   D.   million

5. The symbol > means is   5._____

    A.   different from   B.   greater than
    C.   less than   D.   the same as

6. An order to a person to appear in court at a certain time, as a witness, is known as a(n)   6._____

    A.   affidavit   B.   deposition
    C.   injunction   D.   subpoena

7. A *quire* is a unit used to indicate a certain   7._____

    A.   length of cloth
    B.   length of wire
    C.   number of sheets of paper
    D.   number of vegetables

8. The specific gravity of a liquid may be defined as the ratio of the weight of a given volume of the liquid to the weight of an equal volume of water. An empty bottle weighs 5 oz. When the bottle is filled with water, the total weight is 50 oz. When the bottle is filled with another liquid, the total weight is 95 oz.
The specific gravity of the second liquid is MOST NEARLY   8._____

    A.   .50   B.   .58   C.   1.7   D.   2.0

9. If one inch is approximately equal to 2.54 centimeters, the number of inches in one meter   9.____
   is MOST NEARLY

   A. 14.2   B. 25.4   C. 39.4   D. 91.4

10. If there are 7680 minims in 1 pint and 128 fluid drams in 1 pint, the number of minims in   10.____
    a fluid dram is

    A. 30   B. 60   C. 120   D. 240

Questions 11-25.

DIRECTIONS: For each Question 11 through 25, inclusive, select the option whose meaning
               is MOST NEARLY the same as that of the capitalized word.

11. VARIATION   11.____

    A. change   B. representative
    C. simplification   D. trial

12. CREDIBLE   12.____

    A. believable   B. impossible
    C. payable   D. understandable

13. SUBTERFUGE   13.____

    A. argument   B. deception   C. excuse   D. flight

14. CONCISE   14.____

    A. brief   B. mixed   C. sarcastic   D. split

15. SPURIOUS   15.____

    A. angry   B. evident   C. false   D. odd

16. INCOHERENT   16.____

    A. damaged   B. fearful
    C. inside   D. uncoordinated

17. CORROBORATE   17.____

    A. confirm   B. confuse   C. decay   D. defraud

18. GRATUITY   18.____

    A. favor   B. greeting   C. scheme   D. tip

19. ALTERCATION   19.____

    A. angry dispute   B. recent change
    C. renewal   D. substitution

20. DISCRIMINATE   20.____

    A. involve in crime   B. spread widely
    C. test repeatedly   D. treat differently

21. DIVULGE   21._____

    A. reveal   B. separate   C. share   D. swell

22. EMBARGO   22._____

    A. container   B. license   C. load   D. D, stoppage

23. CENSURE   23._____

    A. anxiety   B. blame   C. middle   D. pause

24. CALIBRATE   24._____

    A. check someone else's calculations
    B. derive a formula to give desired results
    C. make calculations after inaccurate measurements have been taken
    D. mark appropriate graduations on a measuring instrument

25. ASCERTAIN   25._____

    A. authorize   B. determine   C. provide   D. publish

KEY (CORRECT ANSWERS)

1. C		11. A	
2. D		12. A	
3. C		13. B	
4. B		14. A	
5. B		15. C	
6. D		16. D	
7. C		17. A	
8. D		18. D	
9. C		19. A	
10. B		20. B	

21.	A
22.	D
23.	B
24.	D
25.	D

TEST 3

DIRECTIONS: Each question or incomplete statement is followed by several suggested answers or completions. Select the one that BEST answers the question or completes the statement. *PRINT THE LETTER OF THE CORRECT ANSWER IN THE SPACE AT THE RIGHT.*

1. The number of liters in 836 pints is MOST NEARLY   1._____

    A. 104   B. 209   C. 395   D. 836

2. The number of cubic feet in a cubic yard is   2._____

    A. 3   B. 9   C. 27   D. 36

3. A cylindrical tank has inside dimensions as follows: height, 40 feet; diameter, 20 feet. Its volume is MOST NEARLY _____ x 3.1416 cubic feet.   3._____

    A. 800   B. 4000   C. 8000   D. 16000

4. There are approximately 67.2 cubic inches in a dry quart. If the number of cubic inches in a container is given, the method of finding the equivalent number of dry quarts is to   4._____

    A. divide the given number of cubic inches by 67.2
    B. divide the given number of cubic inches by 67.2 x 67.2 x 67.2

    C. multiply the given number of cubic inches by $\dfrac{11}{67.2} \times \dfrac{11}{67.2} \times \dfrac{11}{67.2}$
    D. multiply the given number of cubic inches by 67.2

5. An inspector wishes to test a weight used with a certain scale in a store. Using an accurate balance, he counterbalances with merchandise a standard weight equal to the weight of the merchandise. Then he substitutes the weight to be tested for the standard weight and determines any excess or deficiency, using small standard weights until equilibrium of the scale is again reached.
This method is LIKELY to be   5._____

    A. *correct* because weights are permitted certain tolerances
    B. *correct* because the weight to be tested is being compared with standard weights
    C. *incorrect* because the small weights used by the inspector are likely to be less accurate than the large weights
    D. *incorrect* because the weight to be tested is substituted for a standard weight

6. An inspector is testing the volume of a glass graduate used by a pharmacist. He uses a standard graduate filled with water up to an appropriate mark and pours water from it into the graduate used by the pharmacist. When he reaches the same mark on the pharmacist's graduate, there is some water remaining in the standard graduate.
Of the following, the MOST valid implication that can be made as a result of this test is that   6._____

    A. it cannot be considered a proper test since the marks on the pharmacist's graduate were made by the manufacturer
    B. it cannot be considered a proper test since water was used as the testing fluid
    C. the pharmacist's graduate, when used, is likely to deliver less than the amount indicated by the mark

D. the pharmacist's graduate, when used, is likely to deliver more than the amount indicated by the mark

7. Of the following, the one which is a basic purpose for the inspection of gasoline stations by the Department of Markets is to ensure that   7.____

    A. all the pumps used at the station are of the same type
    B. the consumer receives products as advertised according to brand, trade name, or quality
    C. the prices charged are the same as those in other stations in the vicinity
    D. the station is an official inspection station for the State Department of Motor Vehicles

8. Assume that you and another inspector are assigned to work together on a special project which will take several weeks to complete. You realize, after the first few days, that the other inspector is loafing on the job.
Of the following, the MOST advisable action for you to take is to   8.____

    A. caution the other inspector that unless he does his share of the work, you will have to report the matter to your superior
    B. do as much of the work as you can and say nothing to the other employee or anyone else
    C. limit the amount of work you do to what you consider to be your proper share
    D. report the matter to your superior without further delay

9. Assume that you, as an inspector, disagree with the instructions of your supervisor as to the way a certain job should be done.
Of the following, the MOST advisable action for you to take is to   9.____

    A. ask the supervisor to assign another inspector to do the work
    B. discuss the matter with your supervisor, giving your reasons for your disagreement with his instructions
    C. do the job according to your supervisor's instructions without making any comment
    D. do the job in your own way, if you feel that you can obtain proper results

10. An inspector entering a retail store finds that several boxes and merchandise displays are stacked near one of the scales used in the store. He tells the owner to move this material away from the scale.
Of the following, the MOST probable reason for the inspector's action is that   10.____

    A. customers may be able to have a full view of the scale when making purchases
    B. customers may be detracted from watching the scale by the nearby displays
    C. material stored too near the scale may be pushed over by a customer and possibly injure other customers
    D. material stored too near the scale may possibly fall upon the scale and damage it

11. Of the following statements concerning reports prepared by an inspector, the one which is LEAST valid is: 11.____

    A. Prompt and accurate reports are of value to the work of the unit to which the inspector is assigned but they are of little concern to the operations of the rest of the department

B. Prompt and accurate reports may or may not impress superiors with the necessity for immediate action on their part
C. Reports prepared by inspectors may provide valuable reference material for future activities
D. Reports submitted by an inspector are useful indicators of the efficiency of his work

12. An inspector, after testing a scale in a retail market, finds that it gives short weight. The vendor promises to have the scale repaired immediately.
Of the following, the MOST advisable action for the inspector to take is to

    12._____

A. place a condemned tag on the scale in an inconspicuous spot so as not to embarrass the vendor
B. place a condemned tag on the scale in such a way that anyone can easily see it
C. recommend a good mechanic so that the scale can be properly repaired before he returns later that day
D. tell the vendor that he will return later that day, and if the scale is repaired by then, he will take no further action

13. An inspector is in one of the retail markets supervised by the Department of Markets, He overhears a very loud argument going on between a customer and one of the vendors. The argument is concerned with the price being charged for some merchandise.
Of the following, the MOST advisable action for the inspector to take FIRST is to

    13._____

A. attempt to ignore the incident since he has nothing to do with prices being charged
B. recommend that the vendor be charged with a violation for creating a disturbance in the market
C. tell the patron to leave the market and make his purchase elsewhere if he can't keep quiet
D. try to get the persons involved to settle the argument or quiet down

14. A certain person has made numerous complaints to the Department of Markets to the effect that he has been defrauded by various merchants with whom he has had dealings. In the past, investigation showed that none of his complaints were ever valid and that he is merely a *crank*. Assume that he has come to the office to make another complaint, and, since you happen to be one of the inspectors in the office at the time, you are told to interview him. From your conversation, it appears obvious to you that this is another baseless complaint.
Of the following, the MOST advisable action for you to take is to

    14._____

A. explain to him that there is no point in investigating this complaint since experience has shown that his complaints are always unfounded
B. explain to him that unless he has specific evidence to support his complaint, the department will be unable to take any action
C. tell him that the department will investigate this complaint as it does all others
D. terminate the conversation abruptly and ignore the entire matter

15. Suppose that the operator of a business licensed by the Department of Markets inno-   15.____
cently commits a minor violation of one of the department's regulations.
Of the following, the MOST advisable action for an inspector to take is to

    A. consult his supervisor concerning the action that should be taken in such a case
    B. ignore the matter entirely
    C. ·make sure that the operator understands the appropriate action to take to prevent the recurrence of such violations in the future
    D. report the violation for appropriate penalty despite his feelings about the matter

16. Of the following statements concerning reports submitted by an Inspector of Markets,   16.____
Weights, and Measures, the one which is MOST valid is:

    A. A very detailed report may be of less value than a brief report giving the essential facts
    B. Reports should be considered as confidential, and should be written in such language that they can be understood only by those who are technically trained in the work of the department
    C. Reports should give only the facts. Conclusions and recommendations should be left to the supervisor who reviews them.
    D. The position of the important points in a report will not have much influence on the emphasis placed on them by the reader as long as they are all included

17. Suppose that, as a newly appointed inspector, you are being given field training under   17.____
the guidance of a supervising inspector. On a certain day, you have an appointment to
meet him in the morning at a certain place of business, instead of at the office of the
department. While coming from home, you are delayed a half hour on the subway.
When you leave the subway station, which is some distance fron the meeting place,
the MOST advisable action for you to take FIRST is to

    A. proceed as quickly as possible to the meeting place
    B. return directly to the office
    C. telephone the firm where you are to meet the supervising inspector and ask to speak to him
    D. telephone the office and explain the situation

18. The organization of the Department of Markets includes a bureau which has as one of its   18.____
functions the gathering of information concerning the city's food supply and the prices of
various items of food.
Of the following, the MOST important reason for this activity is that it

    A. can supply interested newspapers or other organizations with desired information
    B. may aid the public in securing proper nutrition at reasonable prices
    C. may supply needed information to producers and shippers of food
    D. supplies statistics which help give a complete picture of food distribution in the city

19. The time when an inspector should be especially watchful for possible short weighing by   19.____
vendors in a supermarket is

    A. during early morning hours when there are likely to be few people in the store to see what is going on
    B. during employees' lunch hour periods when the manager of the store is not likely to be present

    C.   during evening rush hours when business is heavy and there are many people in the store
    D.   just before closing when the store is being prepared for the next day's business

Questions 20-21.

DIRECTIONS: Questions 20 and 21 are to be answered on the basis of the information contained in the following paragraph.

    In all systems of weights and measures based on one or more arbitrary fundamental units, the concrete representation of the unit in the form of a standard is necessary, and the construction and preservation of such a standard is a matter of primary importance. Therefore, it is essential that the standard should be so constructed as to be as nearly permanent and invariable as human ingenuity can contrive. The reference of all measures to an original standard is essential for their correctness, and such a standard must be maintained and preserved in its integrity by some responsible authority which is thus able to provide against the use of false weights and measures. Accordingly, from earliest times, standards were constructed and preserved under the direction of kings and priests, and the temples were a favorite place for their deposit. Later, this duty was assumed by the government, and today, we find the integrity of standards of weights and measures safeguarded by international agreement.

20.   Of the following, the MOST valid implication which can be made on the basis of the above paragraph is that   20.____

    A.   fundamental units of systems of weights and measures should be represented by quantities so constructed that they are specific and constant
    B.   in the earliest times standards were so constructed that they were as permanent and invariable as modern ones
    C.   international agreement has practically relieved the U.S. government of the necessity of preserving standards of weights and measures
    D.   the preservation of standards is of less importance than the ingenuity used in their construction

21.   Of the following, the MOST appropriate title for the above passage is   21.____

    A.   THE CONSTRUCTION AND PRESERVATION OF STANDARDS OF WEIGHTS AND MEASURES
    B.   THE FIXING OF RESPONSIBILITY FOR THE ESTABLISHMENT OF STANDARDS OF WEIGHTS AND MEASURES
    C.   THE HISTORY OF SYSTEMS OF WEIGHTS AND MEASURES
    D.   THE VALUE OF PROPER STANDARDS IN PROVIDING CORRECT WEIGHTS AND MEASURES

Questions 22-23.

DIRECTIONS: Questions 22 and 23 are to be answered on the basis of the information contained in the following paragraph.

    Accurate weighing and good scales insure that excess is not given just for the sake of good measure. No more striking example of the fundamental importance of correct weighing to the business man is found than in the simple and usual relation where a charge or value is obtained by multiplying a weight by a unit price. For example, a scale may weigh *light,* that is, the actual quantity delivered is in excess by 1 percent. The actual result is that the seller taxes himself. If his profit is supposed to be 10 percent of total sales, an overweight of 1 percent represents 10 percent of that profit. Under these conditions, the situation is as though the seller were required to pay a sales tax equivalent to what he is taxing himself.

22. Of the following, the MOST valid implication which can be made on the basis of the above paragraph is that

    A. consistent use of scales that weigh *light* will reduce sellers' profits
    B. no good businessman would give any buyer more than the weight required even if his scale is accurate
    C. the kind of situation described in the above passage could not arise if sales were being made of merchandise sold by the yard
    D. the use of incorrect scales is one of the reasons causing governments to impose sales taxes

22.____

23. According to the above paragraph, the MOST accurate of the following statements is:

    A. If his scale weighs *light* by an amount of 2 percent, the seller would deliver only 98 pounds when 100 pounds was the amount agreed upon
    B. If the seller's scale weighs *heavy,* the buyer will receive an amount in excess of what he intended to purchase
    C. If the seller's scale weighs *light* by an amount of 1 percent, a buyer who agreed to purchase 50 pounds of merchandise would actually receive 50J pounds
    D. The use of a scale which delivers an amount which is in excess of that required is an example of deliberate fraud

23.____

Questions 24-25.

DIRECTIONS: Questions 24 and 25 are to be answered on the basis of the information contained in the following passage.

Food shall be deemed to be misbranded:

1. If its labeling is false or misleading in any particular.

2. If any word, statement or other information required by or under authority of this article to appear on the label or labeling is not prominently placed thereon with such conspicuousness (as compared with other words, statements, designs or devices in the labeling) and in such terms as to render it likely to be read and understood by the ordinary individual under customary conditions of purchase and use.

3. If it purports to be or is represented as a food for which a standard of quality has been prescribed and its quality falls below such standard, unless its label bears a statement that it falls below such standard.

24. According to the above passage, the MOST accurate of the following statements is: 24.____

    A. A food may be considered misbranded if the label contains a considerable amount of information which is not required

    B. If a consumer purchased one type of canned food although he intended to buy another, the food is probably misbranded

    C. If a food is used in large amounts by a group of people of certain foreign origin, it can be considered misbranded unless the label is in the foreign language with which they are familiar

    D. The required information on a label is likely to be in larger print than other information which may appear on it

25. According to the above passage, the one of the following foods which may be considered to be misbranded is a   25.____

    A. can of peaches with a label which carries the brand name of the packer but states *Below Standard in Quality*

    B. can of vegetables with a label on which is printed a shield which states *U.S. Grade B*

    C. package of frozen food which has some pertinent information printed on it in very small type which a customer cannot read and which the store manager cannot read when asked to do so by the customer

    D. package of margarine of the same size as the usual package of butter, kept near the butter, but clearly labeled as margarine

---

KEY (CORRECT ANSWERS)

1.	C		11.	A
2.	C		12.	B
3.	B		13.	D
4.	A		14.	B
5.	B		15.	C
6.	C		16.	A
7.	B		17.	C
8.	A		18.	B
9.	B		19.	C
10.	A		20.	A

21.	D
22.	A
23.	C
24.	D
25.	C

TEST 4

DIRECTIONS: Each question or incomplete statement is followed by several suggested answers or completions. Select the one that BEST answers the question or completes the statement. *PRINT THE LETTER OF THE CORRECT ANSWER IN THE SPACE AT THE RIGHT.*

Questions 1-8.

DIRECTIONS: Questions 1 through 8, inclusive, are based SOLELY on Tables A and B and the notes below.

TABLE A
PURCHASES MADE IN A MEAT MARKET
(Self-Service Refrigerated Meat Case)

ITEM	PRINTED PRICE PER POUND	WEIGHT INDICATED	ACTUAL WEIGHT	PRICE PER PACKAGE
Beef Liver	40¢	1 lb. 2 oz.	1 lb. 2 oz.	50¢
Pork Loins:				
Rib End	29¢	2 lbs. 4 oz.	2 lbs. 1 oz.	66¢
Loin End	32¢	1 lb. 8 oz.	1 lb. 5 oz.	48¢
Veal Chops:				
Shoulder	70¢	2 lbs. 8 oz.	2 lbs. 2 oz.	$1.75
Rib	80¢	1 lb. 10 oz.	1 lb. 12 oz.	$1.50
Loin	90¢	3 lbs. 2 oz.	2 lbs. 10 oz.	$2.05
Flank Steak	88¢	2 lbs. 14 oz.	2 lbs. 3 oz.	$2.53
Cube Steak	80¢	12 oz.	12 oz.	60¢
Top Sirloin Roast	99¢	1 lb. 12 oz.	1 lb. 8 oz.	$1.75
Fresh Ham	55¢	4 lbs. 6 oz.	4 lbs.	$2.40
Bologna	40¢	6 oz.	5 oz.	15¢
Frankfurters	45¢	1 lb, 4 oz.	1 lb. 1 oz.	57¢

TABLE B
PURCHASES MADE IN A CONFECTIONERY

ITEM	PRICE QUOTED PER POUND	AMOUNT REQUESTED	WEIGHTS USED					PRICE CHARGD
			2 lb.	1 lb.	1/2 lb.	1/4 lb.	1 oz.	
Chocolate Almonds	$1.12	3 1/4 lbs.	1	1		1	-	$3.64
Peanut Brittle	$1.09	1 3/4 lbs.	—	1	1	1	—	$1.91
Bridge Mix	$1.25	5 oz.				1	1	$ .40
Special TV Mix	$1.49	2 1/2 lbs.	1	—	1	—	—	$3.75
Choc. Cherries	$1.89	40 pieces	1			1	3	$4.60
Caramels	$1.05	4 lbs.	2	-	-	-	-	$4.20
Cashew Crunch	$1.04	7 lbs.	2	2	1	2	-	$7.28

NOTES

Tables A and B represent hypothetical purchases made in a meat market and in a confectionery. In the case of the meat market, the price and weight figures were taken from the label on each meat package. The label gives the price per pound, the supposed weight of the package, and the price of the package. In answering questions pertaining to the meat market, make no allowance for the weight of wrapping materials.

At the confectionery, all sales are weighed out on an even-balance scale using weights of various sizes. In checking the accuracy of the weights, it was found that the 1 oz. weights did actually weigh 1 oz. each, but that the 1/4 lb. weights weighed 3 oz. each, the 1/2 lb. weights weighed 6 oz. each, the 1 lb. weights weighed 14 oz. each, and the 2 lb. weights weighed 1 lb. 10 oz. each. While the confectionery purchases were being made, note was taken of the weights used in weighing each purchase. The weights which were used are shown in Table B.

If you find, when computing the proper price of a meat or candy item, that the price comes out to a fractional part of a penny, assume that the proprietor is justified in charging a sum equal to the next higher penny. For example, if the computed price of an article is 38 1/4 cents, the proprietor may properly charge 39 cents.

1. If the weight indicated on the package containing veal chops (loin) were accurate, the cost of the package should have been

    A. $2.36   B. $2.75   C. $2.79   D. $2.82

1._____

2. Based on the actual weight, how much should the package of bologna have cost?

    A. 13¢   B. 14¢   C. 16¢   D. 17¢

2._____

3. The purchaser who bought the flank steak package overpaid, on the basis of the actual weight of the package, APPROXIMATELY

    A. 9¢   B. 53¢   C. 60¢   D. 69¢

3._____

4. The actual weight of all of the packages of meat shown in Table A is _____ lbs. _____ oz.

    A. 20; 8   B. 20; 13
    C. 23; 8   D. none of the above

4._____

5. Each chocolate cherry actually weighs APPROXIMATELY _____ oz.

    A. .2   B. .5   C. . 8   D. 1.2

5._____

6. The cashew crunch purchase actually weighted _____ lbs. _____ oz.

    A. 5; 9   B. 5; 12   C. 5; 15   D. D, 6; 2

6._____

7. In accordance with the amount actually received, the chocolate almond purchase should have cost MOST NEARLY

    A. $2.31   B. $2.67   C. $2.80   D. $3.01

7._____

8. Which of the following combinations of weights used by the confectionery would have come CLOSEST to giving the purchaser of the Special TV Mix the weight he requested? 1-2 lb. weight; _____.

    A. 1 1/2 lb. weight
    B. 2 1/2 lb. weight
    C. 2 1/2 lb. weights; 1-1 oz. weight
    D. 2 1/2 lb. weights; 21 oz. weights

8._____

Questions 9-10.

DIRECTIONS: Questions 9 and 10 are to be answered on the basis of the information contained in the following paragraph.

Open Air Markets originally came into existence spontaneously when groups of pushcart
peddlers congregated in spots where business was good. Good business induced them to
return to these spots daily, and, thus, unofficial open air markets arose. These peddlers paid
no fees, and the city received no revenue from them. Confusion and disorder reigned in these
unsupervised markets; the earliest arrivals secured the best locations, unless or until forcibly
ejected by stronger or tougher peddlers. Although the Open Air Markets supplied a definite
need in the community, there were many detrimental factors involved in their operation. They
were unsightly, created unsanitary conditions in market streets by the deposit of garbage and
waste and were a definite obstruction to traffic, as well as a fire hazard.

9.   On the basis of the above paragraph, the MOST accurate of the following statements is: 9._____

   A.   Each peddler in the original open air markets had his own fixed location
   B.   Open air markets were originally organized by means of agreements between
      groups of pushcart peddlers
   C.   The locations of these markets depended upon the amount of business the ven-
      dors were able to do
   D.   There was confusion and disorder in these open air markets because the peddlers
      were not required to pay any fees to the city

10.   Of the following, the MOST valid implication which can be made on the basis of the   10._____
above paragraph is that the

   A.   detrimental aspect of the operations of open air markets was the probable reason
      for the creation of enclosed markets under the supervision of the Department of
      Markets
   B.   open air markets could not supply any community need without proper supervision
   C.   original open air markets were good examples of the operation of fair competition
      in business
   D.   possibility of obtaining a source of revenue was probably the most important rea-
      son for the city's ultimate undertaking of the supervision of open air markets

Questions 11-12.

DIRECTIONS: Questions 11 and 12 are to be answered on the basis of the information contained in the following paragraph.

A person who displays on his window, door, or in his place of business, words or letters in
Hebraic characters other than the word *kosher,* or any sign, emblem, insignia, six-pointed
star, symbol or mark in simulation of same, without displaying in conjunction therewith in
English letters of at least the same size as such characters, signs, emblems, insignia or
marks, the words *we sell kosher meat and food only,* or *we sell non-kosher meat and food
only,* or *we sell both kosher and non-kosher meat and food,* as the case may be, is guilty of a
misdemeanor. Possession of non-kosher meat and food in any place of business advertising
the sale of kosher meat and food only is presumptive evidence that the person in possession
exposes the same for sale with intent to defraud, in violation of the provisions of this section.

11.   Of the following, the MOST valid implication that can be made on the basis of the above   11._____
paragraph is that a person who

A. displays on his window, a six-pointed star in addition to the word *kosher* in Hebraic letters is guilty of intent to defraud

B. displays on his window the word *kosher* in Hebraic characters intends to indicate that he has only kosher food for sale

C. sells both kosher and non-kosher food in the same place of business is guilty of a misdemeanor

D. sells only that type of food which can be characterized as neither kosher nor non-kosher, such as fruit and vegetables, without an explanatory sign in English, is guilty of intent to defraud

12. Of the following, the one which would constitute a violation of the rules of the above paragraph is a case in which a person   12.____

A. displays the word *kosher* on his window in Hebraic letters, has only kosher meat and food in the store but has some non-kosher meat in the rear of the establishment

B. selling both kosher and non-kosher meat and food uses words in Hebraic letters, other than the word *kosher,* on his window and a sign of the same sized letters in English stating, *we sell both kosher and non-kosher meat and food*

C. selling only kosher meat and food uses words in Hebraic letters, other than the word *kosher,* on his window and a sign of the same sized letters in English stating, *we sell kosher meat and food only*

D. selling only non-kosher meat and food displays a six-pointed star on his window and a sign of the same sized letters in English stating, *we sell only non-kosher meat and food*

Questions 13-14.

DIRECTIONS: Questions 13 and 14 are to be answered on the basis of the information contained in the following paragraph.

COMMODITIES IN GLASS BOTTLES OR JARS

The contents of the bottle may be stated in terms of weight or of fluid measure, the weight being indicated in terms of pounds and ounces and the fluid measure being indicated in terms of gallons, quarts, pints, half-pints, gills or fluid ounces. When contents are liquid, the amount should not be stated in terms of weight. The marking indicating content is to be on a tag attached to the bottle or upon a label. The letters shall be in bold-faced type at least one-ninth of an inch (1/9") in height for bottles or jars having a capacity of a gill, half-pint, pint or multiples of a pint, and letters at least three-sixteenths of an inch (3/16") in height for bottles of other capacities, on a part of the tag or label free from other printing or ornamentation, leaving a clear space around the marking which indicates the contents.

13. Of the following, the one which does NOT meet the requirements of the above paragraph is a 13.____

    A. bottle of cooking oil with a label stating *contents -16 fluid ounces* in appropriate sized letters

    B. bottle of vinegar with a label stating contents - *8 ounces avoir* in appropriate sized letters

    C. glass jar filled with instant coffee with a label stating *contents - 1 lb. S oz. avoir* in appropriate sized letters

    D. glass jar filled with liquid bleach with a label stating *contents - 1 quart* in appropriate sized letters

14. Of the following, the one which does meet the requirements of the above paragraph is a 14.____

    A. bottle filled with a low-calorie liquid sweetner with a label stating *contents - S fluid ounces* in letters 1/12" high

    B. bottle filled with ammonia solution for cleaning with a label stating *contents - 1 pint* in letters 1/10" high

    C. jar filled with baking powder with a label stating *contents - 1/2 pint* in letters 1/4" high

    D. jar filled with hard candy with a label stating *contents - 1 lb. avoir* in letters 1/2" high

Question 15.

DIRECTIONS: Question 15 is to be answered on the basis of the information contained in the following passage.

DEALERS IN SECOND HAND DEVICES

1. It shall be unlawful for any person to engage in or conduct the business of dealing in, trading in, selling, receiving, or repairing condemned, rebuilt or used weighing or measuring devices without a permit therefor.

2. Such permit shall expire on the twenty-eighth day of February next succeeding the date of issuance thereof.

3. Every person engaged in the above business, within five days after the making of a repair, or the sale and delivery of a repaired, rebuilt or used weighing or measuring device, shall serve notice in writing on the commissioner giving the name and address of the person for whom the repair has been made or to whom a repaired, rebuilt or used weighing or measuring device has been sold or delivered, and shall include a statement that such device has been so altered, repaired, or rebuilt as to conform to the regulations of the department.

15. According to the above passage, the MOST accurate of the following statements is: 15.____

    A. A permit issued to engage in the business mentioned above, first issued on April 23, 2015, expired on February 29, 2016

    B. A rebuilt or repaired weighing or measuring device should not operate with less error than the tolerances permitted by the regulations of the department

    C. If a used scale in good condition is sold, it is not necessary for the seller to notify the commissioner of the name and address of the buyer

D. There is a difference in the time required to notify the commissioner of a repair or of a sale of a repaired device

Questions 16-17,

DIRECTIONS: Questions 16 and 17 are to be answered on the basis of the information contained in the following passage.

(a) It shall be unlawful for any person, firm or corporation to sell or offer for sale at retail for use in internal combustion engines in motor vehicles any gasoline unless such seller shall post and keep continuously posted on the individual pump or other dispensing device from which such gasoline is sold or offered for sale a sign or placard not less than seven inches in height and eight inches in width nor larger than twelve inches in height and twelve inches in width and stating clearly in numbers of uniform size the selling price or prices per gallon of such gasoline so sold or offered for sale from such pump or other dispensing device.

(b) The amount of governmental tax to be collected in connection with the sale of such gasoline shall be stated on such sign or placard and separately and apart from such selling price or prices.

16. The one of the following price signs posted on a gasoline pump which would be in violation of the above passage is a sign _____ square inches in size and _____ inches high.

    A. 144; 12   B. 84; 7   C. 72; 12   D. 60; 8

16._____

17. According to the above passage, the LEAST accurate of the following statements is:

    A. Gasoline may be sold from a dispensing device other than a pump
    B. If two different pumps are used to sell the same grade of gasoline, a price sign must appear on each pump
    C. The amount of governmental tax and the price of the gasoline must not be stated on the same sign
    D. The sizes of the numbers used on a sign to indicate the price of gasoline must be the same

17._____

18. Although the Live Poultry Law requires that live poultry be sold at the Live Poultry Terminal according to grade, it has been said that such grading is not truly necessary for the business carried on there.
Of the following, the MOST probable reason for this statement is that

    A. it is extremely difficult to determine the grades of live poultry since there are so many factors to be considered in making a determination
    B. supply and demand will determine prices paid by the merchants and dealers operating there and good poultry will naturally bring the highest prices whether it is officially graded or not
    C. the differences between the various grades of live poultry are likely to be so small that they are of little consequence to the ultimate consumer
    D. the standards for grades of live poultry will tend to differ in different parts of the country, and this would lead to confusion when grading is involved in wholesale dealings in poultry

18._____

19. Under the Live Poultry Law, a *Commission Merchant* is defined as: *A person in the busi-ness of receiving live poultry from shippers, farmers, producers or others on consign-ment for sale on their behalf.*
Of the following, the MOST valid assumption that can be made on the basis of the above definition is that the commission merchant

    A. is considered to be the owner of any live poultry he sells at the Live Poultry Termi-nal and returns part of his profit to the shipper, farmer or producer
    B. must guarantee a certain return to the shipper, farmer or producer
    C. must necessarily receive only a fixed percentage of the sales he is able to make at the Live Poultry Terminal
    D. probably makes agreements with shippers, farmers and producers as to how he shall be paid for his services

19.____

20. The regulations of the Live Poultry Law contain restrictions against the feeding of live poultry at the Live Poultry Terminal before sale.
Of the following, the MOST probable reason for such regulations is that

    A. at the terminal it is difficult to maintain the proper sanitary conditions under which poultry should be fed
    B. such feeding would probably result in an increase in weight for which the buyer would pay without receiving proper value for his purchase
    C. the time involved in feeding the poultry would delay transactions at the terminal and interfere with its efficient operation
    D. those who do business at the terminal may not be familiar with the proper type of feed for the poultry and the physical condition of the birds may be affected

20.____

21. One of the functions of the inspectors at the Live Poultry Terminal is to examine the poul-try to see that any birds affected by disease are not offered for sale or sold.
Of the following, the PRINCIPAL reason for such inspection is to

    A. influence shippers, farmers, and producers to take proper measures to prevent poultry from becoming diseased
    B. protect the buyer at the terminal from losing money through the purchase of dis-eased poultry which he may not be able to resell
    C. protect the seller from being accused of offering unfit poultry for sale
    D. protect the ultimate consumer from purchasing poultry which is unfit for human consumption

21.____

22. It shall be unlawful for any person to deal in, receive, buy, sell, give away, distribute or have in his possession dressed poultry which has been processed outside of the city unless such poultry has received ante-mortem inspection and has been approved for condition by the United States Department of Agriculture or the State Department of Agriculture and Markets.
The term *ante-mortem inspection,* as used in the above passage, refers to inspection

    A. after slaughter
    B. before slaughter
    C. by a governmental agency
    D. by the processing plant operator

22.____

23. A squab is a young

   A. female duck
   C. pigeon of either sex

   B. goose of either sex
   D. tom turkey

23.____

24. The one of the following classes of chickens which is youngest in age is a

   A. broiler   B. cock   C. fowl   D. roaster

24.____

25. The guinea is a type of

   A. duck
   B. goose
   C. turkey
   D. poultry different from any of those mentioned above

25.____

KEY (CORRECT ANSWERS)

1.	D	11.	B
2.	A	12.	A
3.	C	13.	B
4.	B	14.	D
5.	C	15.	A
6.	B	16.	C
7.	D	17.	C
8.	D	18.	B
9.	C	19.	D
10.	A	20.	B

21.	D
22.	B
23.	C
24.	A
25.	D

EXAMINATION SECTION
TEST 1

DIRECTIONS: Each question or incomplete statement is followed by several suggested answers or completions. Select the one that BEST answers the question or completes the statement. *PRINT THE LETTER OF THE CORRECT ANSWER IN THE SPACE AT THE RIGHT.*

1. A shop clerk is notified that only 75 bolts can be supplied by Vendor A.
   If this represents 12.5% of the total requisition, then how many bolts were *originally* ordered?

   A. 125   B. 600   C. 700   D. 900

   1.____

2. An enclosed square-shaped storage area with sides of 16 feet each has a safe-load capacity of 250 pounds per square foot.
   The MAXIMUM evenly distributed weight that can be stored in this area is _____ lbs.

   A. 1,056   B. 4,000   C. 64,000   D. 102,400

   2.____

3. A clerical employee has completed 70 progress reports the first week, 87 the second week, and 80 the third week. Assuming a 4-week month, how many progress reports must the clerk complete in the fourth week in order to attain an average of 85 progress reports per week for the month?

   A. 93   B. 103   C. 113   D. 133

   3.____

4. On the first of the month, Shop X received a delivery of 150 gallons of lubricating oil. During the month, the following amounts of oil were used on lubricating work each week: 30 quarts, 36 quarts, 20 quarts, and 48 quarts. The amount of lubricating oil *remaining* at the end of the month was _____ gallons.

   A. 4   B. 33.5   C. 41.5   D. 116.5

   4.____

5. For working a 35-hour week, Employee A earns a gross amount of $480.90. For each hour that Employee A works over 40 hours a week, he is entitled to 1 1/2 times his hourly wage rate.
   If Employee A worked 9 hours on Monday, 8 hours on Tuesday, 9 hours 30 minutes on Wednesday, 9 hours 15 minutes on Thursday, and 9 hours 15 minutes on Friday, what should his *gross* salary be for that week?

   A. $618.30   B. $632.04   C. $652.65   D. $687.00

   5.____

6. An enclosed cube-shaped storage bay has dimensions of 12 feet by 12 feet by 12 feet. Standard procedure requires that there be at least 1 foot of space between the walls, the ceiling, and the stored items.
   What is the MAXIMUM number of cube-shaped boxes with length, width, and height of 1 foot each that can be stored on 1-foot high pallets in this bay?

   A. 1,000   B. 1,331   C. 1,452   D. 1,728

   6.____

7. Assume that two ceilings are to be painted. One ceiling measures 30 feet by 15 feet and the second 45 feet by 60 feet.
   If one quart of paint will cover 60 square feet of ceiling, *approximately* how much paint will be required to paint the two ceilings? _____ gallons.

   7.____

A. 6   B. 10   C. 13   D. 18

8. In last year's budget, $7,500 was spent for office supplies. Of this amount, 60% was spent for paper supplies. If the price of paper has risen 20% over last year's price, then the amount that will be spent this year on paper supplies, assuming the same quantity will be purchased, will be   8.____

A. $3,600   B. $5,200   C. $5,400   D. $6,000

Questions 9-13.

DIRECTIONS: Questions 9 through 13 are to be answered on the basis of the following information.

A certain shop keeps an informational card file on all suppliers and merchandise. On each card is the supplier's name, the contrast number for the merchandise he supplies, and a delivery date for the merchandise. In this filing system, the supplier's name is filed alphabetically, the contract number for the merchandise is filed numerically, and the delivery date is filed chronologically.

In Questions 9 through 13, there are five notations numbered 1 through 5 shown in Column I. Each notation is made up of a supplier's name, a contract number, and a date which is to be filed according to the following rules:

First: File in alphabetical order
Second: When two or more notations have the same supplier, file according to the contract number in numerical order beginning with the lowest number
Third: When two or more notations have the same supplier and contract number, file according to the date beginning with the earliest date.

In Column II, the numbers 1 through 5 are arranged in four ways to show four different orders in which the merchandise information might be filed. Pick the answer (A, B, C, or D) in Column II in which the notations are arranged according to the above filing rules.

SAMPLE QUESTION:

COLUMN I	COLUMN II
1. Cluney (4865) 6/17/05	A. 2, 3, 4, 1, 5
2. Roster (2466) 5/10/04	B. 2, 5, 1, 3, 4
3. Altool (7114) 10/15/05	C. 3, 2, 1, 4, 5
4. Cluney (5276) 12/18/04	D. 3, 5, 1, 4, 2
5. Cluney (4865) 4/8/05	

The CORRECT way to file the cards is:

3. Altool (7114) 10/15/05
5. Cluney (4865) 4/8/05
1. Cluney (4865) 6/17/05
4. Cluney (5276) 12/18/04
2. Roster (2466) 5/10/04

Since the correct filing order is 3, 5, 1, 4, 2, the answer to the sample question is D.

COLUMN I		COLUMN II		
9.	1. Warren (96063) 3/30/06 2. Moore (21237) 9/4/07 3. Newman (10050) 12/12/06 4. Downs (81251) 1/2/06 5. Oliver (60145) 6/30/07	A. 2, 4, 3, 5, 1 B. 2, 3, 5, 4, 1 C. 4, 5, 2, 3, 1 D. 4, 2, 3, 5, 1		9.____
10.	1. Henry (40552) 7/6/07 2. Boyd (91251) 9/1/06 3. George (8196) 12/12/06 4. George (31096) 1/12/07 5. West (6109) 8/9/06	A. 5, 4, 3, 1, 2 B. 2, 3, 4, 1, 5 C. 2, 4, 3, 1, 5 D. 5, 2, 3, 1, 4		10.____
11.	1. Salba (4670) 9/7/06 2. Salba (51219) 3/1/06 3. Crete (81562) 7/1/07 4. Salba (51219) 1/11/07 5. Texi (31549) 1/25/06	A. 5, 3, 1, 2, 4 B. 3, 1, 2, 4, 5 C. 3, 5, 4, 2, 1 D. 5, 3, 4, 2, 1		11.____
12.	1. Crayone (87105) 6/10/07 2. Shamba (49210) 1/5/06 3. Valiant (3152) 5/1/07 4. Valiant (3152) 1/9/07 5. Poro (59613) 7/1/06	A. 1, 2, 5, 3, 4 B. 1, 5, 2, 3, 4 C. 1, 5, 3, 4, 2 D. 1, 5, 2, 4, 3		12.____
13.	1. Mackie (42169) 12/20/06 2. Lebo (5198) 9/12/05 3. Drummon (99631) 9/9/07 4. Lebo (15311) 1/25/05 5. Harvin (81765) 6/2/06	A. 3, 2, 1, 5, 4 B. 3, 2, 4, 5, 1 C. 3, 5, 2, 4, 1 D. 3, 5, 4, 2, 1		13.____

Questions 14-18.

DIRECTIONS: Questions 14 through 18 are to be answered on the basis of the following information.

In order to make sure stock is properly located, incoming units are stored as follows:

Stock Numbers	Bin Numbers
00100 - 39999	D30, L44
40000 - 69999	I4L, D38
70000 - 99999	41L, 80D
100000 and over	614, 83D

Using the above table, choose the answer (A, B, C, or D) which lists the correct bin number for the stock number given.

14. 17243   14.____

    A. 41L   B. 83D   C. I4L   D. D30

15. 9219   15.____

    A. D38   B. L44   C. 614   D. 41L

16. 90125   16.____

    A. 41L   B. 614   C. D38   D. D30

17. 10001   17.____

    A. L44   B. D38   C. SOD   D. 83D

18. 200100   18.____

    A. 41L   B. I4L   C. 83D   D. D30

19. A supervisor believes that the current filing systems used in his office are not efficient.   19.____
When his superior goes on vacation, he intends to change all the filing procedures.
For a supervisor to undertake this move without his superior's knowledge would GEN-
ERALLY be considered

    A.   *advisable;* it shows that he has initiative
    B.   *inadvisable;* the current filing systems are probably the best
    C.   *advisable;* the result will be an increase in productivity
    D.   *inadvisable;* the supervisor should be informed of any intended changes

20. Assume that you have been assigned the task of handling all telephone calls at a sanita-   20.____
tion garage. After a recent snowstorm, your supervisor informed you that all available
personnel have been assigned to snow removal duties. However, you have been receiving numerous telephone calls from the public in regard to unshoveled streets and intersections.
In handling these calls, it is generally considered good policy by the department to

    A.   indicate to the callers that the department is clearing streets off as quickly as pos-
sible
    B.   tell the callers there is nothing that can be done
    C.   tell the callers that they are tying up departmental telephones with needless com-
plaints
    D.   promise the callers that streets will be cleared by the evening

———

KEY (CORRECT ANSWERS)

1.	B	11.	B
2.	C	12.	D
3.	B	13.	C
4.	D	14.	D
5.	C	15.	B
6.	A	16.	A
7.	C	17.	A
8.	C	18.	C
9.	D	19.	D
10.	B	20.	A

———

TEST 2

DIRECTIONS: Each question or incomplete statement is followed by several suggested answers or completions. Select the one that BEST answers the question or completes the statement. *PRINT THE LETTER OF TEE CORRECT ANSWER IN THE SPACE AT THE RIGHT.*

Questions 1-10.

DIRECTIONS: Questions 1 through 10 are to be answered on the basis of the following information.

A code number for any item is obtained by combining the date of delivery, number of units received, and number of units used.

The first two digits represent the day of the month, the third and fourth digits represent the month, and the fifth and sixth digits represent the year.

The number following the letter R represents the number of units received and the number following the letter U represents the number of units used.

For example, the code number 120673-R5690-U1001 indicates that a delivery of 5,690 units was made on June 12, of which 1,001 units were used.

Using the chart below, answer Questions 1 through 6 by choosing the letter (A, B, C, or D) in which the supplier and stock number correspond to the code number given.

Supplier	Stock Number	Number of Units Received	Delivery Date	Number of Units Used
Stony	38390	8300	May 11	3800
Stoney	39803	1780	September 15	1703
Nievo	21220	5527	October 10	5007
Nieve	38903	1733	August 5	1703
Monte	39213	5527	October 10	5007
Stony	38890	3308	December 9	3300
Stony	83930	3880	September 12	380
Nevo	47101	485	June 11	231
Nievo	12122	5725	May 11	5201
Neve	47101	9721	August 15	8207
Nievo	21120	2275	January 7	2175
Rosa	41210	3821	March 3	2710
Stony	38890	3308	September 12	3300
Dinal	54921	1711	April 2	1117
Stony	33890	8038	March 5	3300
Dinal	54721	1171	March 2	717
Claridge	81927	3308	April 5	3088
Nievo	21122	4878	June 7	3492
Haley	39670	8300	December 23	5300

1. Code No. 120972-R3308-U3300   1._____

   A. Nievo - 12122   B. Stony - 83930
   C. Nievo - 21220   D. Stony - 38890

2. Code No. 101072-R5527-U5007   2.____

    A. Nievo - 21220   B. Haley - 39670
    C. Monte - 39213   D. Claridge - 81927

3. Code No. 101073-R5527-U5007   3.____

    A. Nievo - 21220   B. Monte - 39213
    C. Nievo - 12122   D. Nievo - 21120

4. Code No. 110573-R5725-U5201   4.____

    A. Nievo - 12122   B. Nievo - 21220
    C. Haley - 39670   D. Stony - 38390

5. Code No. 070172-R2275-U2175   5.____

    A. Stony - 33890   B. Stony - 83930
    C. Stony - 38390   D. Nievo - 21120

6. Code No. 120972-R3880-U380   6.____

    A. Stony - 83930   B. Stony - 38890
    C. Stony - 33890   D. Monte - 39213

Using the same chart, answer Questions 7 through 10, choosing the letter (A, B, C, or D) in which the code number corresponds to the supplier and stock number given.

7. Nieve - 38903   7.____

    A. 951973-R1733-U1703   B. 080572-R1733-U1703
    C. 080573-R1733-U1703   D. 050873-R1733-U1703

8. Nevo - 47101   8.____

    A. 081573-R9721-U8207   B. 091573-R9721-U8207]
    C. 110672-R485-U231   D. 061172-R485-U231

9. Dinal - 54921   9.____

    A. 020473-R1711-U1117   B. 030272-R1171-U717
    C. 020372-R1171-U717   D. 421973-R1711-U1117

10. Nievo - 21122   10.____

    A. 070672-R4878-U3492   B. 060772-R4878-U349
    C. 761972-R4878-U3492   D. 060772-R4878-U3492

11. A citizen who has called the office at which you are working has started yelling on the   11.____
telephone. He is annoyed because he has been switched from office to office and still
has not reached the proper party.
Of the following, the BEST practice to follow is to

    A. hang up on this individual since he is obviously a troublemaker
    B. yell back at him for being so childish
    C. tell him that you have heard that complaint before
    D. try to calm this person and help him reach the proper party

12. Which of the following is the MOST likely result of employees publicly criticizing the activ-   12.____
    ities of their agency?
    The

    A. employees will be terminated for the good of the agency
    B. public's respect for the agency may decrease
    C. productive members of the agency may resign
    D. agency may sue these employees for libel

13. It is essential for city employees who deal with the public to provide service as promptly   13.____
    and completely as possible.
    Letters from the public lodging complaints regarding poor service should GENERALLY
    be handled by

    A. answering them as soon as possible according to agency procedures
    B. ignoring them, since only troublemakers usually write such letters
    C. returning them, since the city government does not respond to public complaints
    D. acknowledging them with no further action necessary

14. While checking the work of a clerk who is under your supervision, you notice that he has   14.____
    made the same mistake a number of times.
    In order to help prevent this clerk from making the same mistake again, it would be
    BEST for you to take which of the following courses of action?

    A. Correct the errors yourself and not mention it to the clerk
    B. Provide training for the clerk
    C. Reprimand the clerk for the mistakes made
    D. Remind the clerk of the errors he has previously made

15. A community resident calls the sanitation garage in which you are working to inquire   15.____
    about the days in which old furniture can be put on the street for collection. Although your
    unit is responsible for these collections, you do not have this information and there is
    nobody in the office to assist you.
    Of the following, it would be MOST advisable to

    A. tell the citizen to call back in an hour
    B. get the citizen's telephone number and inform him that you will call back when you
       get the information
    C. switch the call to another unit and let them get the information
    D. put the caller on hold and try to find someone that has the answer

16. As a supervisor, you have been given the responsibility of maintaining attendance   16.____
    records for your garage. A co-worker, who has been late a number of times, has asked
    you to overlook his recent lateness since it involves only ten minutes. He has been
    warned previously for lateness and will receive some kind of disciplinary action because
    of this recent lateness, for you to overlook the lateness would be

    A. *advisable;* it involves only a matter of ten minutes
    B. *inadvisable;* this employee should have to suffer the consequences of his actions
    C. *advisable;* morale in the unit will improve
    D. *inadvisable;* employee lateness should never be excused

17. When a supervisor answers incoming telephone calls, it is important for him to FIRST   17.____

    A. identify himself and/or his office
    B. ask the caller to state the reason for the call
    C. ask the caller the nature of the call
    D. ask the caller to identify himself

18. It appears to you that the current mail distribution procedures are inefficient.   18.____
    For you to make a suggestion to your supervisor for the implementation of new proce-
    dures, would be

    A. *advisable;* if the supervisor thinks your ideas are worthwhile;they may be imple-
       mented
    B. *inadvisable;* supervisors generally are not interested in changing procedures
    C. *advisable;* new procedures generally provide better results than old procedures
    D. *inadvisable;* only methods analysts should suggest changes in procedures

19. As a supervisor, you direct the work of two clerks. Recently, you discovered that one of   19.____
    the two clerks generally loafs around on Friday afternoons. This past Friday, you saw this
    particular employee standing around conversing with several employees. At that point,
    you severely reprimanded this employee in the presence of the other employees.
    For you to have reprimanded this employee in such a fashion was

    A. *advisable;* this employee *had it coming*
    B. *inadvisable;* you should have spoken to him privately
    C. *advisable;* this reprimand also served as a warning to the others
    D. *inadvisable;* employees should not be reprimanded

20. As a supervisor, you have been assigned to maintain garage supplies. Recently, a co-   20.____
    worker requested a quantity of nails and screws for use in his home. Since this involves
    only a small amount of supplies, he felt it would not be wrong to make such a request.
    In this case, it would be ADVISABLE for you to

    A. give the co-worker the supplies
    B. remind the co-worker that city supplies are only for city use
    C. notify the investigation department in regard to this employee
    D. forget the incident

KEY (CORRECT ANSWERS)

1.	D	11.	D
2.	C	12.	B
3.	A	13.	A
4.	A	14.	B
5.	D	15.	B
6.	A	16.	B
7.	D	17.	A
8.	C	18.	A
9.	A	19.	B
10.	A	20.	B

EXAMINATION SECTION
TEST 1

DIRECTIONS: Each question or incomplete statement is followed by several suggested answers or completions. Select the one that BEST answers the question or completes the statement. *PRINT THE LETTER OF THE CORRECT ANSWER IN THE SPACE AT THE RIGHT.*

1. Good procedure in handling complaints from the public may be divided into the following four principal stages:

     I.   Investigation of the complaint
     II.   Receipt of the complaint
     III.   Assignment of responsibility for investigation and correction
     IV.   Notification of correction

The ORDER in which these stages ordinarily come is:

   A. III, II, I, IV   B. II, III, I, IV
   C. II, III, IV, I   D. II, IV, III, I

1.____

2. The department may expect the MOST severe public criticism if

   A. it asks for an increase in its annual budget
   B. it purchases new and costly street cleaning equipment
   C. sanitation officers and men are reclassified to higher salary grades
   D. there is delay in cleaning streets of snow

2.____

3. The MOST important function of public relations in the department should be to

   A. develop cooperation on the part of the public in keeping streets clean
   B. get stricter penalties enacted for health code violations
   C. recruit candidates for entrance positions who can be developed into supervisors
   D. train career personnel so that they can advance in the department

3.____

4. The one of the following which has MOST frequently elicited unfavorable public comment has been

   A. dirty sidewalks or streets
   B. dumping on lots
   C. failure to curb dogs
   D. overflowing garbage cans

4.____

5. It has been suggested that, as a public relations measure, sections hold *open house* for the public.
The MOST effective time for this would be

   A. during the summer when children are not in school and can accompany their parents
   B. during the winter when snow is likely to fall and the public can see snow removal preparations
   C. immediately after a heavy snow storm when department snow removal operations are in full progress
   D. when street sanitation is receiving general attention as during *Keep City Clean* week

5.____

6. When a public agency conducts a public relations program, it is MOST likely to find that each recipient of its message will

    A. disagree with the basic purpose of the message if the officials are not well known to him

    B. accept the message if it is presented by someone perceived as having a definite intention to persuade

    C. ignore the message unless it is presented in a literate and clever manner

    D. give greater attention to certain portions of the message as a result of his individual and cultural differences

6._____

7. Following are three statements about public relations and communications:

    I. A person who seeks to influence public opinion can speed up a trend

    II. Mass communications is the exposure of a mass audience to an idea

    III. All media are equally effective in reaching opinion leaders

Which of the following choices CORRECTLY classifies the above statements into those which are correct and those which are not?

    A. I and II are correct, but III is not

    B. II and III are correct, but I is not

    C. I and III are correct, but II is not

    D. III is correct, but I and II are not

7._____

8. Public relations experts say that MAXIMUM effect for a message results from

    A. concentrating in one medium

    B. ignoring mass media and concentrating on *opinion makers*

    C. presenting only those factors which support a given position

    D. using a combination of two or more of the available media

8._____

9. To assure credibility and avoid hostility, the public relations man MUST

    A. make certain his message is truthful, not evasive or exaggerated

    B. make sure his message contains some dire consequence if ignored

    C. repeat the message often enough so that it cannot be ignored

    D. try to reach as many people and groups as possible

9._____

10. The public relations man MUST be prepared to assume that members of his audience

    A. may have developed attitudes toward his proposals --favorable, neutral, or unfavorable

    B. will be immediately hostile

    C. will consider his proposals with an open mind

    D. will invariably need an introduction to his subject

10._____

11. The one of the following statements that is CORRECT is:

    A. When a stupid question is asked of you by the public, it should be disregarded

    B. If you insist on formality between you and the public, the public will not be able to ask stupid questions that cannot be answered

    C. The public should be treated courteously, regardless of how stupid their questions may be

    D. You should explain to the public how stupid their questions are

11._____

12. With regard to public relations, the MOST important item which should be emphasized in
an employee training program is that

    A. each inspector is a public relations agent
    B. an inspector should give the public all the information it asks for
    C. it is better to make mistakes and give erroneous information than to tell the public
that you do not know the correct answer to their problem
    D. public relations is so specialized a field that only persons specially trained in it
should consider it

12._____

13. Members of the public frequently ask about departmental procedures.
Of the following, it is BEST to

    A. advise the public to put the question in writing so ,that he can get a proper formal
reply
    B. refuse to answer because this is a confidential matter
    C. explain the procedure as briefly as possible
    D. attempt to avoid the issue by discussing other matters

13._____

14. The effectiveness of a public relations program in a public agency such as the authority
is BEST indicated by the

    A. amount of mass media publicity favorable to the policies of the authority
    B. morale of those employees who directly serve the patrons of the authority
    C. public's understanding and support of the authority's program and policies
    D. number of complaints received by the authority from patrons using its facilities

14._____

15. In an attempt to improve public opinion about a certain idea, the BEST course of action
for an agency to take would be to present the

    A. clearest statements of the idea even though the language is somewhat technical
    B. idea as the result of long-term studies
    C. idea in association with something familiar to most people
    D. idea as the viewpoint of the majority leaders

15._____

16. The fundamental factor in any agency's community relations program is

    A. an outline of the objectives
    B. relations with the media
    C. the everyday actions of the employees
    D. a well-planned supervisory program

16._____

17. The FUNDAMENTAL factor in the success of a community relations program is

    A. true commitment by the community
    B. true commitment by the administration
    C. a well-planned, systematic approach
    D. the actions of individuals in their contacts with the public

17._____

18. The statement below which is LEAST correct is:

    A. Because of selection standards, the supervisor frequently encounters problems
resulting from subordinates' inability to express themselves in the language of the
profession

18._____

B. Distortion of the meaning of a communication is usually brought about by a failure to use language that has a precise meaning to others

C. The term *filtering* is the distortion or dilution of content of a communication that occurs as information is passed from individual to individual

D. The complexity of the *communications net* will directly affect

19. Consider the following three statements that may or may not be CORRECT: 19._____
    I. In order to prevent the stifling of communications flow, supervisors should insist that employees use the formal communications network
    II. Two-way communications are faster and more accurate than one-way communications
    III. There is a direct correlation between the effectiveness of communications and the total setting in which they occur
The choice below which MOST accurately describes the above statement is:

A. All 3 are correct
B. All 3 are incorrect
C. More than one of the statements is correct
D. Only one of the statements is correct

20. The statement below which is MOST inaccurate is: 20._____

A. The supervisor's most important tool in learning whether or not he is communicating well is feedback
B. Follow-up is essential if useful feedback is to be obtained
C. Subordinates are entitled, as a matter of right, to explanations from management concerning the reasons for orders or directives
D. A skilled supervisor is often able to use the grapevine to good advantage

21. *Since concurrence by those affected is not sought, this kind of communication can be*   21._____
issued with relative ease. The kind of communication being referred to in this quotation is

A. autocratic   B. democratic   C. directive   D. free-rein

22. The statement below which is LEAST correct is: 22._____

A. Clarity is more important in oral communicating than in written since the readers of a written communication can read it over again
B. Excessive use of abbreviations in written communications should be avoided
C. Short sentences with simple words are preferred over complex sentences and difficult words in a written communication
D. The *newspaper* style of writing ordinarily simplifies expression and facilitates understanding

23. Which one of the following is the MOST important factor for the department to consider in   23._____
building a good public image?

A. A good working relationship with the news media
B. An efficient community relations program
C. An efficient system for handling citizen complaints
D. The proper maintenance of facilities and equipment
E. The behavior of individuals in their contacts with the public

24. It has been said that the ability to communicate clearly and concisely is the MOST impor- 24.____
    tant single skill of the supervisor.
    Consider the following statements:
    I.   The adage, *Actions speak louder than words,* has NO application in superior/
         subordinate communications since good communications are accomplished
         with words
    II. The environment in which a communication takes place will *rarely* determine
         its effect
    III. Words are symbolic representations which must be associated with past
         experience or else they are meaningless
    The choice below which MOST accurately describes the above statements is:

    A. I, II and III are correct
    B. I and II are correct, but III is not
    C. I and III are correct, but II is not
    D. III is correct, but I and II are not
    E. I, II, and III are incorrect

25. According to expert opinion, the effectiveness of an organization is very dependent upon 25.____
    good upward, downward, and lateral communications. Lateral communications are most
    important to the activity of coordinating the efforts of organizational units. Before real
    communication can take place at any level, barriers to communication must be recog-
    nized, understood, and removed. Consider the following three statements:
    I.   The *principal* barrier to good communications is a failure to establish empa-
         thy between sender and receiver
    II. The difference in status or rank between the sender and receiver of a com-
         munication may be a communications barrier
    III. Communications are easier if they travel upward from subordinate to supe-
         rior
    The choice below which MOST accurately describes the above statements is:

    A. I, II and III are incorrect
    B. I and II are incorrect
    C. I, II, and III are correct
    D. I and II are correct
    E. I and III are incorrect

KEY (CORRECT ANSWERS)

1.	B		11.	C
2.	D		12.	A
3.	A		13.	C
4.	A		14.	C
5.	D		15.	C
6.	D		16.	C
7.	A		17.	D
8.	D		18.	A
9.	A		19.	D
10.	A		20.	C

21.	A
22.	A
23.	E
24.	D
25.	E

READING COMPREHENSION
UNDERSTANDING WRITTEN MATERIALS
COMMENTARY

The ability to read and understand written materials – texts, publications, newspapers, orders, directions, expositions – is a skill basic to a functioning democracy and to an efficient business or viable government.

That is why almost all examinations – for beginning, middle, and senior levels – test reading comprehension, directly or indirectly.

The reading test measures how well you understand what you read. This is how it is done: You read a passage followed by several statements. From these statements, you choose the *one* statement, or answer, that is BEST supported by, or BEST matches, what is said in the paragraph. *PRINT THE LETTER OF THE CORRECT ANSWER IN THE SPACE AT THE RIGHT.*

SAMPLE QUESTION

DIRECTIONS: Answer Question 1 ONLY according to the information given in the following passage :

1.   A cashier has to make many arithmetic calculations in connection with his work. Skill in arithmetic comes readily with practice; no special talent is needed.
On the basis of the above statement, it is MOST accurate to state that

    A.   the most important part of a cashier's job is to make calculations
    B.   few cashiers have the special ability needed to handle arithmetic problems easily
    C.   without special talent, cashiers cannot learn to do the calculations they are required to do in their work
    D.   a cashier can, with practice, learn to handle the computations he is required to make.

The *correct* answer is D.

1.____

EXAMINATION SECTION
TEST 1

Questions 1-5.

DIRECTIONS: Questions 1 to 5 are based on the following reading passage:

The size of each collection route will be determined by the amount of waste per stop, distance between stops, speed of loading, speed of truck, traffic conditions during loading time, etc.

Basically, the route should consist of a proper amount of work for a crew for the daily working period. The crew should service all properties eligible for this service in their area. Routes should, whenever practical, be compact, with a logical progression through the area. Unnecessary travel should be avoided. Traffic conditions on the route should be thoroughly studied to prevent lost time in loading, to reduce hazards to employees, and to minimize tying up of regular traffic movements by collection forces. Natural and physical barriers and arterial streets should be used as route boundaries wherever possible to avoid lost time in travel.

Routes within a district should be laid out so that the crews start at the point farthest from the disposal area and, as the day progresses, move toward that area, thus reducing the length of the haul. When possible, the work of the crews in a district should be parallel as they progress throughout the day, with routes finishing up within a short distance of each other. This enables the supervisor to be present when crews are completing their work and enables him to shift crews to trouble spots to complete the day's work.

1. Based on the above passage, an advantage of having collection routes end near one another is that

    A. routes can be made more compact
    B. unnecessary travel is avoided, saving manpower
    C. the length of the haul is reduced
    D. the supervisor can exercise better manpower control

1._____

2. Of the factors mentioned above which affect the size of a collection route, the two over which the sanitation forces have LEAST control are

    A. amount of waste; traffic conditions
    B. speed of loading; amount of waste
    C. speed of truck; distance between stops
    D. traffic conditions; speed of truck

2._____

3. According to the above passage, the size of a collection route is probably good if

    A. it is a fair day's work for a normal crew
    B. it is not necessary for the trucks to travel too fast
    C. the amount of waste collected can be handled properly
    D. the distance between stops is approximately equal

3._____

4. Based on the above passage, it is reasonable to assume that a sanitation officer laying out collection routes should NOT try to have

    4.____

    A.   an arterial street as a route boundary
    B.   any routes near the disposal area
    C.   the routes overlap a little
    D.   the routes run in the same direction

5. The term "logical progression" as used in the second paragraph of the passage refers MOST nearly to

    5.____

    A.   collecting from street after street in order
    B.   numbering streets one after the other
    C.   rotating crew assignments
    D.   using logic as a basis for assignment of crews

TEST 2

DIRECTIONS: Answer Questions 1, 2, and 3 *SOLELY* on the basis of the paragraph below.

In an open discussion designed to arrive at solutions to community problems, the person leading the discussion group should give the members a chance to make their suggestions before he makes his. He must not be afraid of silence, if he talks just to keep things going, he will find he can't stop, and good discussion will not develop. In other words, the more he talks, the more the group will depend on him. If he finds, however, that no one seems ready to begin the discussion, his best "opening" is to ask for definitions of terms which form the basis of the discussion. By pulling out as many definitions or interpretations as possible, he can get the group started "thinking out loud," which is essential to good discussion.

1. According to the above paragraph, good group discussion is *most likely* to result if the person leading the discussion group   1.____

   A. keeps the discussion going by speaking whenever the group stops speaking
   B. encourages the group to depend on him by speaking more than any other group member
   C. makes his own suggestions before the group has a chance to make theirs
   D. encourages discussion by asking the group to interpret the terms to be discussed

2. According to the paragraph above, "thinking out loud" by the discussion group is   2.____

   A. *good* practice, because "thinking out loud" is important to good discussion
   B. *poor* practice, because group members should think out their ideas before discussing them
   C. *good* practice, because it will encourage the person leading the discussion to speak more
   D. *poor* practice, because it causes the group to fear silence during a discussion

3. According to the paragraph above, the *one* of the following which is LEAST desirable at an open discussion is having   3.____

   A. silent periods during which none of the group members speaks
   B. differences of opinion among the group members concerning the definition of terms
   C. a discussion leader who uses "openings" to get the discussion started
   D. a discussion leader who provides all suggestions and definitions for the group

———

TEST 3

Questions 1-4.

DIRECTIONS: Questions 1 through 4 are to be answered *SOLELY* on the basis of the following information.

The insects you will control are just a minute fraction of the millions which inhabit the world. Man does well to hold his own in the face of the constant pressures that insects continue to exert upon him. Not only are the total numbers tremendous, but the number of individual kinds, or species, certainly exceeds 800,000 — number greater than that of all other animals combined. Many of these are beneficial but some are especially competitive with man. Not only are insects numerous, but they are among he most adaptable of all animals. In their many forms, they are fitted for almost any specific way of life. Their adaptability, combined with their tremendous rate of reproduction, gives insects an unequaled potential for survival!

The food of insects includes almost anything that can be eaten by any other animal as well as many things which cannot even be digested by any other animals. Most insects do not harm the products of man or carry diseases harmful to him; however many do carry diseases and others feed on his food and manufactured goods. Some are adapted to living only in open areas while others are able to live in extremely confined spaces. All of these factors combined make the insects a group of animals having many members which are a nuisance to man and thus of great importance.

The control of insects requires an understanding of their way of life. Thus it is necessary to understand the anatomy of the insect, its method of growth, the time it takes for the insect to grow from egg to adult, its habits, the stage of its life history in which it causes damage, its food, and its common living places. In order to obtain the best control, it is especially important to be able to identify correctly the specific insect involved because, without this knowledge, it is impossible to prescribe a proper treatment.

1. Which one of the following is a CORRECT statement about the insect population of the world, according to the above paragraph? The

    A. total number of insects is less than the total number of all other animals combined
    B. number of species of insects is greater than the number of species of all other animals combined
    C. total number of harmful insects is greater than the total number of those which are not harmful
    D. number of species of harmless insects is less than the number of species of those which are harmful

2. Insects will be controlled MOST efficiently if you

    A. understand why the insects are so numerous
    B. know what insects you are dealing with
    C. see if the insects compete with man
    D. are able to identify the food which the insects digest

3. According to the above passage, insects are of importance to a scientist **PRIMARILY**   3.____
   because they

    A. can be annoying, destructive, and harmful to man
    B. are able to thrive in very small spaces
    C. cause damage during their growth stages
    D. are so adaptable that they can adjust to any environment

4. According to the above passage, insects can eat   4.____

    A. everything that any other living thing can eat
    B. man's food and things which he makes
    C. anything which other animals can't digest
    D. only food and food products

———

TEST 4

Questions 1-4.

DIRECTIONS: Answer Questions 1 through 4 on the basis of the information given in the following passage.

Telephone service in a government agency should be adequate and complete with
respect to information given or action taken. It must be remembered that telephone contacts
should receive special consideration since the caller cannot see the operator. People like to
feel that they are receiving personal attention and that their requests or criticisms are receiving individual rather than routine consideration. All this contributes to what has come to be
known as *tone of service*. The aim is to use standards which are clearly very good or superior. The factors to be considered in determining what makes good tone of service are
speech, courtesy, understanding and explanations. A caller's impression of tone of service
will affect the general public attitude toward the agency and city services in general.

1.   The above passage states that people who telephone a government agency like to feel   1.____
     that they are

     A.   creating a positive image of themselves
     B.   being given routine consideration
     C.   receiving individual attention
     D.   setting standards for telephone service

2.   Which of the following is NOT mentioned in the above passage as a factor in determining   2.____
     good tone of service?

     A.   Courtesy   B.   Education   C.   Speech   D.   Understanding

3.   The above passage implies that failure to properly handle telephone calls is *most likely* to   3.____
     result in

     A.   a poor impression of city agencies by the public
     B.   a deterioration of courtesy toward operators
     C.   an effort by operators to improve the Tone of Service
     D.   special consideration by the public of operator difficulties

---

TEST 5

Questions 1-5.

DIRECTIONS: Answer Questions 1 through 5 only on the basis of the information provided in the following passage:

For some office workers it is useful to be familiar with the four main classes of domestic mail; for others it is essential. Each class has a different rate of postage and some have requirements concerning wrapping, sealing or special information to be placed on the package.

First-class mail, the class which may not be opened for postal inspection, includes letters, post cards, business reply cards, and other kinds of written matter. There are different rates for some of the kinds of cards which can be sent by first-class mail. The maximum weight for an item sent by first-class mail is 70 pounds. An item which is not letter size should be marked "First Class" on all sides.

Although office workers most often come into contact with first-class mail, they may find it helpful to know something about the other classes. Second-class mail is generally used for mailing newspapers and magazines. Publishers of these articles must meet certain U.S. Postal Service requirements in order to obtain a permit to use second-class mailing rates. Third-class mail, which must weigh less than 1 pound, includes printed materials and merchandise parcels. There are two rate structures for this class, a single-piece rate and a bulk rate. Fourth-class mail, also known as parcel post, includes packages weighing from one to 40 pounds. For more information about these classes of mail and the actual mailing rates, contact your local post office.

1. According to this passage, first-class mail is the only class which   1.____

    A. has a limit on the maximum weight of an item
    B. has different rates for items within the class
    C. may not be opened for postal inspection
    D. should be used by office workers

2. According to this passage, the one of the following items which may CORRECTLY be sent by fourth-class mail is a   2.____

    A. magazine weighing one-half pound
    B. package weighing one-half pound
    C. package weighing two pounds
    D. post card

3. According to this passage, there are different postage rates for   3.____

    A. a newspaper sent by second-class mail and a magazine sent by second-class mail
    B. each of the classes of mail
    C. each pound of fourth-class mail
    D. printed material sent by third-class mail and merchandise parcels sent by third-class mail

4. In order to send a newspaper by second-class mail, a publisher must   4.____

    A. have met certain postal requirements and obtained a permit
    B. indicate whether he wants to use the single-piece or the bulk rate
    C. make certain that the newspaper weighs less than one pound
    D. mark the newspaper "Second Class" on the top and bottom of the wrapper

5. Of the following types of information the one which is NOT mentioned in the passage is   5.____
the

    A. class of mail to which parcel post belongs
    B. kinds of items which can be sent by each class of mail
    C. maximum weight for an item sent by fourth-class mail
    D. postage rate for each of the four classes of mail

TEST 6

DIRECTIONS: Questions numbered 1 to 5 inclusive are to be answered in accordance with the following paragraph.

The thickness of insulation necessary for the most economical results varies with the steam temperature. The standard covering consists of 85 percent magnesia with 10 percent of long-fibre asbestos as a binder. Both matnesia and laminated asbestos-felt and other forms of mineral wool including glass wool are also used for heat insulation. The magnesia and laminated-asbestos coverings may be safely used at temperatures up to 600° F. Pipe insulation is applied in molded sections 3 feet long; the sections are attached to the pipe by means of galvanized iron wire or netting. Flanges and fittings can be insulated by direct application of magnesia cement to the metal without *reinforcement*. Insulation should always be maintained in good condition because it saves fuel. Routine maintenance of warm-pipe insulation should include prompt repair of damaged surfaces. Steam and hot-water leaks concealed by insulation will be difficult to detect. Underground steam or hot-water pipes are best insulated using a concrete trench with removable cover.

1.   The word *reinforcement*, as used above, means, most nearly,   1.____

   A.   resistance   B.   strengthening   C.   regulation   D.   removal

2.   According to the above paragraph, magnesia and laminated asbestos coverings may be   2.____
   safely used at temperatures up to

   A.   800° F   B.   720° F   C.   675° F   D.   600° F

3.   According to the above paragraph, insulation should *always* be maintained in good con-   3.____
   dition because it

   A.   is laminated   B.   saves fuel
   C.   is attached to the pipe   D.   prevents leaks

4.   According to the above paragraph, pipe insulation sections are attached to the pipe by   4.____
   means of

   A.   binders   B.   mineral wool
   C.   netting   D.   staples

5.   According to the above paragraph, a leak in a hot-water pipe may be difficult to detect   5.____
   because, when insulation is used, the leak is

   A.   underground   B.   hidden
   C.   routine   D.   cemented

TEST 7

Questions 1-4.

DIRECTIONS: Questions 1 to 4 inclusive are to be answered *only* in accordance with the following paragraph.

Cylindrical surfaces are the most common form of finished surfaces found on machine parts, although flat surfaces are also very common; hence, many metal-cutting *processes* are for the purpose of producing either cylindrical or flat surfaces. The machines used for cylindrical or flat shapes may be, and often are, utilized also for forming the various irregular or special shapes required on many machine parts. Because of the prevalence of cylindrical and flat surfaces, the student of manufacturing practice should learn first about the machines and methods employed to produce these surfaces. The cylindrical surfaces may be internal as in holes and cylinders. Any one part may, of course, have cylindrical sections of different diameters and lengths and include flat ends or shoulders and, frequently, there is a threaded part or, possibly, some finished surface that is not circular in cross-section. The prevalence of cylindrical surfaces on machine parts explains why lathes are found in all machine shops. It is important to understand the various uses of the lathe because many of the operations are the same fundamentally as those performed on other types of machine tools.

1. According to the above paragraph, the *most common* form of finished surfaces found on machine parts is   1.____

   A. cylindrical   B. elliptical
   C. flat   D. square

2. According to the above paragraph, *any one* part of cylindrical surfaces may have   2.____

   A. chases   B. shoulders   C. keyways   D. splines

3. According to the above paragraph, lathes are found in all machine shops because cylindrical surfaces on machine parts are   3.____

   A. scarce   B. internal   C. common   D. external

4. As used in the above paragraph, the word *processes* means   4.____

   A. operations   B. purposes   C. devices   D. tools

TEST 8

DIRECTIONS: Questions 1 and 2 are to be answered in accordance with the following paragraph.

The principle of interchangeability requires manufacture to such specification that component parts of a device may be selected at random and assembled to fit and operate satisfactorily. Interchangeable manufacture, therefore, requires that parts be made to definite limits of error, and to fit gages instead of mating parts. Interchangeability does not necessarily involve a high degree of precision; stove lids, for example, are interchangeable but are not particularly accurate, and carriage bolts and nuts are not precision products but are completely interchangeable. Interchangeability may be employed in unit-production as well as mass-production systems of manufacture.

1. According to the above paragraph, in order for parts to be interchangeable, they must be   1.____

    A. precision-machined
    C. mass-produced
    B. selectively-assembled
    D. made to fit gages

2. According to the above paragraph, carriage bolts are interchangeable because they are   2.____

    A. precision-made
    B. sized to specific tolerances
    C. individually matched products
    D. produced in small units

KEY (CORRECT ANSWERS)

TEST 1	TEST 2	TEST 3	TEST 4	TEST 5	TEST 6	TEST 7	TEST 8
1. D	1. D	1. B	1. C	1. C	1. B	1. A	1. D
2. A	2. A	2. B	2. B	2. C	2. D	2. B	2. B
3. A	3. D	3. A	3. A	3. B	3. B	3. C	
4. C		4. B	4. B	4. A	4. C	4. A	
5. A				5. D	5. B		

NAME and NUMBER COMPARISONS

COMMENTARY

This test seeks to measure your ability and disposition to do a job carefully and accurately, your attention to exactness and preciseness of detail, your alertness and versatility in discerning similarities and differences between things, and your power in systematically handling written language symbols.

It is actually a test of your ability to do academic and/or clerical work, using the basic elements of verbal (qualitative) and mathematical (quantitative) learning - words _and_ numbers.

EXAMINATION SECTION
TEST 1

DIRECTIONS: In each line across the page there are three names or numbers that are much alike. Compare the three names or numbers and decide which ones are exactly alike. _PRINT IN THE SPACE AT THE RIGHT THE LETTER:_
A.   if all THREE names or numbers are exactly ALIKE
B.   if only the FIRST and SECOND names or numbers are ALIKE
C.   if only the FIRST and THIRD names or numbers are ALIKE
D.   if only the SECOND and THIRD names or numbers are ALIKE
E.   if ALL THREE names or numbers are DIFFERENT

1. Davis Hazen	David Hozen	David Hazen	1._____
2. Lois Appel	Lois Appel	Lois Apfel	2._____
3. June Allan	Jane Allan	Jane Allan	3._____
4. 10235	10235	10235	4._____
5. 32614	32164	32614	5._____

TEST 2

1. 2395890	2395890	2395890	1._____
2. 1926341	1926347	1926314	2._____
3. E. Owens McVey	E. Owen McVey	E. Owen McVay	3._____
4. Emily Neal Rouse	Emily Neal Rowse	Emily Neal Rowse	4._____
5. H. Merritt Audubon	H. Merriott Audubon	H. Merritt Audubon	5._____

TEST 3

1.	6219354	6219354	6219354	1._____
2.	2312793	2312793	2312793	2._____
3.	1065407	1065407	1065047	3._____
4.	Francis Ransdell	Frances Ramsdell	Francis Ramsdell	4._____
5.	Cornelius Detwiler	Cornelius Detwiler	Cornelius Detwiler	5._____

TEST 4

1.	6452054	6452654	6542054	1._____
2.	8501268	8501268	8501286	2._____
3.	Ella Burk Newham	Ella Burk Newnham	Elena Burk Newnham	3._____
4.	Jno. K. Ravencroft	Jno. H. Ravencroft	Jno. H. Ravencoft	4._____
5.	Martin Wills Pullen	Martin Wills Pulen	Martin Wills Pullen	5._____

TEST 5

1.	3457988	3457986	3457986	1._____
2.	4695682	4695862	4695682	2._____
3.	Stricklund Kaneydy	Sticklund Kanedy	Stricklund Kanedy	3._____
4.	Joy Harlor Witner	Joy Harloe Witner	Joy Harloe Witner	4._____
5.	R.M.O. Uberroth	R.M.O. Uberroth	R.N.O. Uberroth	5._____

TEST 6

1.	1592514	1592574	1592574	1._____
2.	2010202	2010202	2010220	2._____
3.	6177396	6177936	6177396	3._____
4.	Drusilla S. Ridgeley	Drusilla S. Ridgeley	Drusilla S. Ridgeley	4._____
5.	Andrei I. Toumantzev	Andrei I. Tourmantzev	Andrei I. Toumantzov	5._____

TEST 7

1.	5261383	5261383	5261338	1._____
2.	8125690	8126690	8125609	2._____
3.	W.E. Johnston	W.E. Johnson	W.E. Johnson	3._____
4.	Vergil L. Muller	Vergil L. Muller	Vergil L. Muller	4._____
5.	Atherton R. Warde	Asheton R. Warde	Atherton P. Warde	5._____

TEST 8

1.	013469.5	023469.5	02346.95	1._____
2.	33376	333766	333766	2._____
3.	Ling-Temco-Vought	Ling-Tenco-Vought	Ling-Temco Vought	3._____
4.	Lorilard Corp.	Lorillard Corp.	Lorrilard Corp.	4._____
5.	American Agronomics Corporation	American Agronomics Corporation	American Agronomic Corporation	5._____

TEST 9

1.	436592864	436592864	436592864	1.____
2.	197765123	197755123	197755123	2.____
3.	Dewaay, Cortvriendt International S.A.	Deway, Cortvriendt International S.A.	Deway, Corturiendt International S.A.	3.____
4.	Crédit Lyonnais	Crèdit Lyonnais	Crèdit Lyonais	4.____
5.	Algemene Bank Nederland N.V.	Algamene Bank Nederland N.V.	Algemene Bank Naderland N.V.	5.____

TEST 10

1.	00032572	0.0032572	00032522	1.____
2.	399745	399745	398745	2.____
3.	Banca Privata Finanziaria S.p.A.	Banca Privata Finanzaria S.P.A.	Banca Privata Finanziaria S.P.A.	3.____
4.	Eastman Dillon, Union Securities & Co.	Eastman Dillon, Union Securities Co.	Eastman Dillon, Union Securities & Co.	4.____
5.	Arnhold and S. Bleichroeder, Inc.	Arnhold & S. Bleichroeder, Inc.	Arnold and S. Bleichroeder, Inc.	5.____

TEST 11

DIRECTIONS: Answer the questions below on the basis of the following instructions: For each such numbered set of names, addresses and numbers listed in Columns I and II, select your answer from the following options:
- A: The names in Columns I and II are different
- B: The addresses in Columns I and II are different
- C: The numbers in Columns I and II are different
- D: The names, addresses and numbers are identical

1. Francis Jones
62 Stately Avenue
96-12446

Francis Jones
62 Stately Avenue
96-21446

1.____

2. Julio Montez
19 Ponderosa Road
56-73161

Julio Montez
19 Ponderosa Road
56-71361

2.____

3. Mary Mitchell
2314 Melbourne Drive
68-92172

Mary Mitchell
2314 Melbourne Drive
68-92172

3.____

4. Harry Patterson
25 Dunne Street
14-33430

Harry Patterson
25 Dunne Street
14-34330

4.____

5. Patrick Murphy
171 West Hosmer Street
93-81214

Patrick Murphy
171 West Hosmer Street
93-18214

5.____

TEST 12

1. August Schultz
816 St. Clair Avenue
53-40149

August Schultz
816 St. Claire Avenue
53-40149

1.____

2. George Taft
72 Runnymede Street
47-04033

George Taft
72 Runnymede Street
47-04023

2.____

3. Angus Henderson
1418 Madison Street
81-76375

Angus Henderson
1418 Madison Street
81-76375

3.____

4. Carolyn Mazur
12 Riven/lew Road
38-99615

Carolyn Mazur
12 Rivervane Road
38-99615

4.____

5. Adele Russell
1725 Lansing Lane
72-91962

Adela Russell
1725 Lansing Lane
72-91962

5.____

TEST 13

DIRECTIONS: The following questions are based on the instructions given below. In each of the following questions, the 3-line name and address in Column I is the master-list entry, and the 3-line entry in Column II is the information to be checked against the master list.

If there is one line that is *not* exactly alike, mark your answer A.
If there are two lines *not* exactly alike, mark your answer B.
If there are three lines *not* exactly alike, mark your answer C.
If the lines *all are* exactly alike, mark your answer D.

1. Jerome A. Jackson   Jerome A. Johnson   1._____
    1243 14th Avenue   1234 14th Avenue
    New York, N.Y. 10023   New York, N.Y. 10023

2. Sophie Strachtheim   Sophie Strachtheim   2._____
    33-28 Connecticut Ave.   33-28 Connecticut Ave.
    Far Rockaway, N.Y. 11697   Far Rockaway, N.Y. 11697

3. Elisabeth NT. Gorrell   Elizabeth NT. Gorrell   3._____
    256 Exchange St   256 Exchange St.
    New York, N.Y. 10013   New York, N.Y. 10013

4. Maria J. Gonzalez   Maria J. Gonzalez   4._____
    7516 E. Sheepshead Rd.   7516 N. Shepshead Rd.
    Brooklyn, N.Y. 11240   Brooklyn, N.Y. 11240

5. Leslie B. Brautenweiler   Leslie B. Brautenwieler   5._____
    21-57A Seller Terr.   21-75ASeilerTerr.
    Flushing, N.Y. 11367   Flushing, N.J. 11367

KEYS (CORRECT ANSWERS)

TEST 1	TEST 2	TEST 3	TEST 4	TEST 5	TEST 6	TEST 7
1. E	1. A	1. A	1. E	1. D	1. D	1. B
2. B	2. E	2. A	2. B	2. C	2. B	2. E
3. D	3. E	3. B	3. E	3. E	3. C	3. D
4. A	4. D	4. E	4. E	4. D	4. A	4. A
5. C	5. C	5. A	5. C	5. B	5. E	5. E

TEST 8	TEST 9	TEST 10	TEST 11	TEST 12	TEST 13
1. E	1. A	1. E	1. C	1. B	1. B
2. D	2. D	2. B	2. C	2. C	2. D
3. E	3. E	3. E	3. D	3. D	3. B
4. E	4. E	4. C	4. C	4. B	4. A
5. B	5. E	5. E	5. C	5. A	5. C

NAME AND NUMBER CHECKING
EXAMINATION SECTION
TEST 1

DIRECTIONS: Each question or incomplete statement is followed by several suggested answers or completions. Select the one that *BEST* answers the question or completes the statement. *PRINT THE LETTER OF THE CORRECT ANSWER IN THE SPACE AT THE RIGHT.*

Questions 1-10

DIRECTIONS: Questions 1 through 10 below present the identification numbers, initials, and last names of employees enrolled in a city retirement system. You are to choose the option (A, B, C, or D) that has the *identical* identification number, initials, and last name as those given in each question.

SAMPLE QUESTION

B145698 JL Jones
  A.   B146798 JL Jones
  C.   P145698 JL Jones

  B.   B145698 JL Jonas
  D.   B145698 JL Jones

The correct answer is D. Only option D shows the identification number, initials and last name exactly as they are in the sample question. Options A, B, and C have errors in the identification number or last name.

1.   J297483 PL Robinson   1._____

  A.   J294783 PL Robinson
  C.   J297483 PI Robinson

  B.   J297483 PL Robinson
  D.   J297843 PL Robinson

2.   S497662 JG Schwartz   2._____

  A.   S497662 JG Schwarz
  C.   S497662 JG Schwartz

  B.   S497762 JG Schwartz
  D.   S497663 JG Schwartz

3.   G696436 LN Alberton   3._____

  A.   G696436 LM Alberton
  C.   G696346 LN Albertson

  B.   G696436 LN Albertson
  D.   G696436 LN Alberton

4.   R774923 AD Aldrich   4._____

  A.   R774923 AD Aldrich
  C.   R774932 AP Aldrich

  B.   R744923 AD Aldrich
  D.   R774932 AD Allrich

5.   N239638 RP Hrynyk   5._____

  A.   N236938 PR Hrynyk
  C.   N239638 PR Hrynyk

  B.   N236938 RP Hrynyk
  D.   N239638 RP Hrynyk

6.   R156949 LT Carlson   6._____

  A.   R156949 LT Carlton
  C.   R159649 LT Carlton

  B.   R156494 LT Carlson
  D.   R156949 LT Carlson

7. T524697 MN Orenstein   7.____

    A. T524697 MN Orenstein   B. T524967 MN Orinstein
    C. T524697 NM Ornstein   D. T524967 NM Orenstein

8. L346239 JD Remsen   8.____

    A. L346239 JD Remson   B. L364239 JD Remsen
    C. L346329 JD Remsen   D. L346239 JD Remsen

9. P966438 SB Rieperson   9.____

    A. P996438 SB Reiperson   B. P966438 SB Reiperson
    C. R996438 SB Rieperson   D. P966438 SB Rieperson

10. D749382 CD Thompson   10.____

    A. P749382 CD Thompson   B. D749832 CD Thomsonn
    C. D749382 CD Thompson   D. D749823 CD Thomspon

Questions 11 - 20

DIRECTIONS: Each of Questions 11 through 20 gives the identification number and name of a person who has received treatment at a certain hospital. You are to choose the option (A, B, C, or D) which has *EXACTLY* the same identification number and name as those given in the question.

SAMPLE QUESTION

123765 Frank Y. Jones

    A. 123675 Frank Y. Jones
    B. 123765 Frank T. Jones
    C. 123765 Frank Y. Johns
    D. 123765 Frank Y. Jones

The correct answer is D. Only option D shows the identification number and name exactly as they are in the sample question. Option A has a mistake in the identification number. Option B has a mistake in the middle initial of the name. Option C has a mistake in the last name.

Now answer Questions 11 through 20 in the same manner.

11. 754898 Diane Malloy

    A. 745898 Diane Malloy   11.____
    B. 754898 Dion Malloy
    C. 754898 Diane Malloy
    D. 754898 Diane Maloy

12. 661818 Ferdinand Figueroa

    A. 661818 Ferdinand Figeuroa   12.____
    B. 661618 Ferdinand Figueroa
    C. 661818 Ferdnand Figueroa
    D. 661818 Ferdinand Figueroa

13. 100101 Norman D. Braustein

    A. 100101 Norman D. Braustein   13.____
    B. 101001 Norman D. Braustein
    C. 100101 Norman P. Braustien
    D. 100101 Norman D. Bruastein

14. 838696 Robert Kittredge

    A. 838969 Robert Kittredge
    B. 838696 Robert Kittredge
    C. 388696 Robert Kittredge
    D. 838696 Robert Kittridge

14._____

15. 243716 Abraham Soletsky

    A. 243716 Abrahm Soletsky
    B. 243716 Abraham Solestky
    C. 243176 Abraham Soletsky
    D. 243716 Abraham Soletsky

15._____

16. 981121 Phillip M. Maas

    A. 981121 Phillip M. Mass
    B. 981211 Phillip M. Maas
    C. 981121 Phillip M. Maas
    D. 981121 Phillip N. Maas

16._____

17. 786556 George Macalusso

    A. 785656 George Macalusso
    B. 786556 George Macalusso
    C. 786556 George Maculasso
    D. 786556 George Macluasso

17._____

18. 639472 Eugene Weber

    A. 639472 Eugene Weber
    B. 639472 Eugene Webre
    C. 693472 Eugene Weber
    D. 639742 Eugene Weber

18._____

19. 724936 John J. Lomonaco

    A. 724936 John J. Lomanoco
    B. 724396 John J. Lomonaco
    C. 724936 John J. Lomonaco
    D. 724936 John J. Lamonaco

19._____

20. 899868 Michael Schnitzer

    A. 899868 Micheal Schnitzer
    B. 898968 Michael Schnizter
    C. 899688 Michael Schnitzer
    D. 899868 Michael Schnitzer

20._____

Questions: 21 - 28

DIRECTIONS: Questions 21 through 28 consist of lines of names, dates, and numbers which represent the names. membership dates, social security numbers, and members of the retirement system.For each question you are to choose the option (A, B, C, or D) in Column II which *EXACTLY* matches the information in Column I.

SAMPLE QUESTION

Column I

Column II

Crossen 12/23/56 173568929 253492

    A. Crossen 2/23/56 173568929 253492
    B. Crossen 12/23/56 173568729 253492
    C. Crossen 12/23/56 173568929 253492
    D. Crossan 12/23/56 173568929 258492

The correct answer is C. Only option C shows the name, date, and numbers exactly as they are in Column I. Option A has a mistake in the date. Option B has a mistake in the social security number. Option D has a mistake in the name and in the membership number.

21. Figueroa 1/15/64 119295386 147563   21.____

    A. Figueroa   1/5/64   119295386   147563
    B. Figueroa   1/15/64   119295386   147563
    C. Figueroa   1/15/64   119295836   147563
    D. Figueroa   1/15/64   119295886   147563

22. Goodridge 6/19/59 106237869 128352   22.____

    A. Goodridge   6/19/59   106287869   128332
    B. Goodrigde   6/19/59   106237869   128352
    C. Goodridge   6/9/59   106237869   128352
    D. Goodridge   6/19/59   106237869   128352

23. Balsam 9/13/57 109652382 116938   23.____

    A. Balsan   9/13/57   109652382   116938
    B. Balsam   9/13/57   109652382   116938
    C. Balsom   9/13/57   109652382   116938
    D. Balsalm   9/13/57   109652382   116938

24. Mackenzie 2/16/49 127362513 101917   24.____

    A. Makenzie   2/16/49   127362513   101917
    B. Mackenzie   2/16/49   127362513   101917
    C. Mackenzie   2/16/49   127362513   101977
    D. Mackenzie   2/16/49   127862513   101917

25. Halpern 12/2/73 115206359 286070   25.____

    A. Halpern   12/2/73   115206359   286070
    B. Halpern   12/2/73   113206359   286070
    C. Halpern   12/2/73   115206359   206870
    D. Halpern   12/2/73   115206359   286870

26. Phillips 4/8/66 137125516 192612   26.____

    A. Phillips   4/8/66   137125516   196212
    B. Philipps   4/8/66   137125516   192612
    C. Phillips   4/8/66   137125516   192612
    D. Phillips   4/8/66   137122516   192612

27. Francisce 11/9/63 123926037 152210   27.____

    A. Francisce   11/9/63   123826837   152210
    B. Francisce   11/9/63   123926037   152210
    C. Francisce   11/9/63   123936037   152210
    D. Franscice   11/9/63   123926037   152210

28.   Silbert 7/28/54 118421999 178514   28._____

    A.   Silbert   7/28/54   118421999   178544
    B.   Silbert   7/28/54   184421999   178514
    C.   Silbert   7/28/54   118421999   178514
    D.   Siblert   7/28/54   118421999   178514

KEY (CORRECT ANSWERS)

1.	B	16.	C
2.	C	17.	B
3.	D	18.	A
4.	A	19.	C
5.	D	20.	D
6.	D	21.	B
7.	A	22.	D
8.	D	23.	B
9.	D	24.	B
10.	C	25.	A
11.	C	26.	C
12.	D	27.	B
13.	A	28.	C
14.	B		
15.	D		

TEST 2

Questions 1-3

DIRECTIONS: Items 1 to 3 are a test of your proofreading ability. Each item consists of Copy I and Copy II. You are to assume that Copy I in each item is correct. Copy II, which is meant to be a duplicate of Copy I, may contain some typographical errors. In each item, compare Copy II with Copy I and determine the number of errors in Copy II. If there are:
no errors, mark your answer A;
1 or 2 errors, mark your answer B;
3 or 4 errors, mark your answer C;
5 or 6 errors, mark your answer D;
7 errors or more, mark your answer E.

1.
1.____

COPY I

The Commissioner, before issuing any such license, shall cause an investigation to be made of the premises named and described in such application, to determine whether all the provisions of the sanitary code, building code, state industrial code, state minimum wage law, local laws, regulations of municipal agencies, and other requirements of this article are fully observed. (Section B32-169.0 of Article 23.)

COPY II

The Commissioner, before issuing any such license shall cause an investigation to be made of the premises named and described in such applecation, to determine whether all the provisions of the sanitary code, bilding code, state industrial code, state minimum wage laws, local laws, regulations of municipal agencies, and other requirements of this article are fully observed. (Section E32-169.0 of Article 23.)

2.
2.____

COPY I

Among the persons who have been appointed to various agencies are John Queen, 9 West 55th Street, Brooklyn; Joseph Blount, 2497 Durward Road, Bronx: Lawrence K. Eberhardt, 3194 Bedford Street, Manhattan; Reginald L. Darcy, 1476 Allerton Drive, Bronx; and Benjamin Ledwith, 177 Greene Street, Manhattan.

COPY II

Among the persons who have been appointed to various agencies are John Queen, 9 West 56th Street, Brooklyn, Joseph Blount, 2497 Dureward Road, Bronx: Lawrence K. Eberhart , 3194 Belford Street, Manhattan; Reginald L. Barcey, 1476 Allerton drive, Bronx; and Benjamin Ledwith, 177 Green Street, Manhattan.

3.
3.____

COPY I

Except as hereinafter provided, it shall be unlawful to use, store or have on hand any inflammable motion picture film in quantities greater than one standard or two sub-standard reels, or aggregating more than two thousand feet in length, or more than ten pounds in weight without the permit required by this section.

COPY II

Except as herinafter provided, it shall be unlawfull to use, store or have on hand any inflamable motion picture film, in quantities greater than one standard or two substandard reels or aggregating more than two thousand feet in length, or more then ten pounds in weight without the permit required by this section.

Questions 4-6

Questions 4 to 6 are a test of your proofreading ability. Each question consists of Copy I and Copy II. You are to assume that Copy I in each question is correct. Copy II, which is meant to be a duplicate of Copy I, may contain some typographical errors. In each question, compare Copy II with Copy I and determine the number of errors in Copy II. If there are

no errors, mark your answer A;
1 or 2 errors, mark your answer B;
3 or 4 errors, mark your answer C;
5 errors or more, mark your answer D.

4.   4.___

COPY I

It shall be unlawful to install wires or appliances for electric light, heat or power, operating at a potential in excess of seven hundred fifty volts, in or on any part of a building, with the exception of a central station, sub-station, transformer, or switching vault, or motor room; provided, however, that the Commissioner may authorize the use of radio transmitting apparatus under special conditions.

COPY II

It shall be unlawful to install wires or appliances for electric light, heat or power, operating at a potential in excess of seven hundred fifty volts, in or on any part of a building, with the exception of a central station, sub-station, transformer, or switching vault, or motor room, provided, however, that the Commissioner may authorize the use of radio transmitting apperatus under special conditions.

5.   5.___

COPY I

The grand total debt service for the fiscal year 2006-07 amounts to $350,563,718.63, as compared with $309,561,347.27 for the current fiscal year, or an increase of $41,002,371.36. The amount payable from other sources in 2006-07 shows an increase of $13,264,165.47, resulting in an increase of $27,733,205.89 payable from tax levy funds.

COPY II

The grand total debt service for the fiscal year 2006-07 amounts to $350,568,718.63, as compared with $309,561,347.27 for the current fiscel year, or an increase of $41,002,371.36. The amount payable from other sources in 2006-07 show an increase of $13,264,165.47 resulting in an increase of $27,733,295.89 payable from tax levy funds.

6.   6._____

<u>COPY I</u>

The following site proposed for the new building is approximately rectangular in shape and comprises an entire block, having frontages of about 721 feet on 16th Road, 200 feet on 157th Street, 721 feet on 17th Avenue and 200 feet on 154th Street, with a gross area of about 144,350 square feet. The 2006-07 assessed valuation is $28,700,000 of which $6,000,000 is for improvements.

<u>COPY II</u>

The following site proposed for the new building is approximately rectangular in shape and comprises an entire block, having frontage of about 721 feet on 16th Road, 200 feet on 157th Street, 721 feet on 17th Avenue, and 200 feet on 134th Street, with a gross area of about 114,350 square feet. The 2006-07 assessed valuation is $28,700,000 of which $6,000,000 is for improvements.

———

KEY (CORRECT ANSWERS)

1. D
2. E
3. E
4. B
5. D
6. C

———

TEST 3

Questions 1-8

DIRECTIONS: Each of the Questions numbered 1 through 8 consists of three sets of names and name codes. In each question, the two names and name codes on the same line are supposed to be exactly the same.

Look carefully at each set of names and codes and mark your answer

    A.   if there are mistakes in all three sets
    B.   if there are mistakes in two of the sets
    C.   if there is a mistake in only one set
    D.   if there are no mistakes in any of the sets

SAMPLE QUESTION

The following sample question is given to help you understand the procedure

Macabe, John N. - V 53162	Macade, John N. - V 53162
Howard, Joan S. - J 24791	Howard, Joan S. - J 24791
Ware, Susan B. - A 45068	Ware, Susan B. - A 45968

In the above sample question, the names and name codes of the first set are not exactly the same because of the spelling of the last name (Macabe - Macade). The names and name codes of the second set are exactly the same. The names and name codes of the third set are not exactly the same because the two name codes are different (A 45068 - A 45968). Since there are mistakes in only 2 of the sets, the answer to the sample question is B.

1.   Powell, Michael C. - 78537 F   Powell, Michael C. - 78537 F   1._____
     Martinez, Pablo J. - 24435 P   Martinez, Pablo J. - 24435 P
     MacBane, Eliot M. - 98674 E   MacBane, Eliot M. - 98674 E

2.   Fitz-Kramer Machines Inc.   Fitz-Kramer Machines Inc.   2._____
            - 259090   - 259090
     Marvel Cleaning Service   Marvel Cleaning Service
            - 482657   - 482657
     Donato, Carl G. - 637418   Danato, Carl G. - 687418

3.   Martin Davison Trading Corp.   Martin Davidson Trading Corp.   3._____
            - 43108 T   - 43108 T
     Cotwald Lighting Fixtures   Cotwald Lighting Fixtures
            - 76065 L   - 70056 L
     R. Crawford Plumbers   R. Crawford Plumbers
            - 23157 C   - 23157 G

4. Fraiman Engineering Corp.
       - M4773
Neuman, Walter B. - N7745
Pierce, Eric M. - W6304
	Friaman Engineering Corp.
	       - M4773
	Neumen, Walter B. - N7745
	Pierce, Eric M. - W6304
		4._____

5. Constable, Eugene - B 64837 Derrick, Paul - H 27119 Heller, Karen - S 49606	Comstable, Eugene - B 64837 Derrik, Paul - H 27119 Heller, Karen - S 46906	5._____

6. Hernando Delivery Service Co.
       - D 7456
Barettz Electrical Supplies
       - N 5392
Tanner, Abraham - M 4798
	Hernando Delivery Service Co.
	       - D 7456
	Barettz Electrical Supplies
	       - N 5392
	Tanner, Abraham - M 4798
		6._____

7. Kalin Associates - R 38641
Sealey, Robert E. - P 63533
Seals! Office Furniture
       - R36742
	Kaline Associates - R 38641
	Sealey, Robert E. - P 63553
	Seals! Office Furniture
	       - R36742
		7._____

8. Janowsky, Philip M.- 742213
Hansen, Thomas H. - 934816
L. Lester and Son Inc.
       – 294568
	Janowsky, Philip M.- 742213
	Hanson, Thomas H. - 934816
	L. Lester and Son Inc.
	       - 294568
		8._____

Questions 9-13

DIRECTIONS: Each of the questions number 9 through 13 consists of three sets of names and building codes. In each question, the two names and building codes on the same line are supposed to be exactly the same.

If you find an error or errors on only *one* of the sets in the question, mark your answer A; any *two* of the sets in the question, mark your answer B; all *three* of the sets in the question, mark your answer C; *none* of the sets in the question, mark your answer D.

Column I
Duvivier, Anne P. - X52714
Dyrborg, Alfred - B4217
Dymnick, JoAnne - P482596

Column II
Duviver, Anne P. - X52714
Dyrborg, Alfred - B4267
Dymnick, JoAnne - P482596

In the above sample question, the first set of names and building codes is not exactly the same because the last names are spelled differently (Duvivier - Duviver). The second set of names and building codes is not exactly the same because the building codes are different (B4217 - B4267). The third set of names and building codes is exactly the same. Since there are mistakes in two of the sets of names and building codes, the answer to the sample question is B.

Now answer the questions on the following page using, the same procedure.

Column I	Column II	
9. Lautmann, Gerald G. - C2483 Lawlor, Michael - W44639 Lawrence, John J. - H1358	Lautmann, Gerald C. - C2483 Lawler, Michael - W44639 Lawrence, John J. - H1358	9.____
10. Mittmann, Howard - J4113 Mitchell, William T.- M75271 Milan, T. Thomas - Q67533	Mittmann, Howard - J4113 Mitchell, William T.- M75271 Milan, T. Thomas - Q67553	10.____
11. Quarles, Vincent - J34760 Quinn, Alan N. - S38813 Quinones, Peter W. - B87467	Quarles, Vincent - J34760 Quinn, Alan N. - S38813 Quinones, Peter W. - B87467	11.____
12. Daniels, Harold H. - A26554 Dantzler, Richard - C35780 Davidson, Martina - E62901	Daniels, Harold H - A26544 Dantzler, Richard - 035780 Davidson, Martin - E62901	12.____
13. Graham, Cecil J. - I20244 Granger, Deborah - T86211 Grant, Charles L. - G5788	Graham, Cecil J. - I20244 Granger, Deborah - T86211 Grant, Charles L. - G5788	13.____

KEY (CORRECT ANSWERS)

1.	D	8.	C
2.	C	9.	B
3.	A	10.	A
4.	B	11.	D
5.	A	12.	C
6.	D	13.	D
7.	B		

TEST 4

Questions 1-9

DIRECTIONS: In questions 1 to 10 there are five pairs of numbers or letters and numbers. Compare each pair and decide how many pairs are *EXACTLY ALIKE*. *PRINT THE LETTER OF THE CORRECT ANSWER IN THE SPACE AT THE RIGHT.*

    A. if only one pair is exactly alike
    B. if only two pairs are exactly alike
    C. if only three pairs are exactly alike
    D. if only four pairs are exactly alike
    E. if all five pairs are exactly alike

1.   73-F......F-73   FF-73. . . .FF-73   1.____
      F-7373....F-7373 373-FF...337-FF
      F-733.....337-F

2.   0-17158. . ..0-17158   0-71518 ... 0-71518   2.____
      0-11758....0-11758   0-15817... 0-15817
      0-51178....0-51178

3.   1A-7908....1A-7908   7A-8901....7A-8091   3.____
      7A-891.....7A-891   1A-9078....1A-9708.
      9A-7018....9A-7081

4.   2V-6426....2V-6246   2N-6246....2N-6246   4.____
      2V-6426....2N-6426   2N-6624....2N-6624
      2V-6462....2V-6462

5.   3NY-56......3ny-65   5NY-356.....3NY-356   5.____
      6NY-3566....3ny-3566 5NY-6536....5NY-6536
      3NY-5663....5ny-3663

6.   COB-065....COB-065 BCL-506....BCL-506   6.____
      LBC-650....LBC-650   DLB-560....DLB-560
      CDB-056....COB-065

7.   4KQ-9130....4KQ-9130 4KQ-9310....4KQ-9130   7.____
      4KQ-9031....4KQ-9031 4KQ-9301....4KQ-9301
      4KQ-9013....4KQ-9013

8.   MK-89......MK-98   98-MK......89-MK   8.____
      MSK-998........MSK-998 MOSK.......MOKS
      SMK-899....SMK-899

9.   8MD-2104....SMD-2014 2MD-8140....2MD-8140   9.____
      814-MD......814-MD   4MD-8201. . . .4MD-8201
      MD-281......MD-481

10. 161-035. .. .161-035 150-316.... 150-316   10.____
      315-160....315-160   131-650....131-650
      165-301....165-301

KEY (CORRECT ANSWERS)

1. B
2. E
3. B
4. C
5. A

6. D
7. D
8. B
9. C
10. E

TEST 5

DIRECTIONS: Each question or incomplete statement is followed by several suggested answers or completions. Select the one that *BEST* answers the question or completes the statement. *PRINT THE LETTER OF THE CORRECT ANSWER IN THE SPACE AT THE RIGHT.*

Questions 1-5

DIRECTIONS: Questions 1 through 5, inclusive, consist of groups of four displays representing license identification plates. Examine each group of plates and determine the number of plates in each group which are identical. Mark your answer sheets as follows:
If only two plates are identical, mark answer A.
If only three plates are identical, mark answer B.
If all four plates are identical, mark answer C.
If the plates are all different, mark answer D

EXAMPLE
ABC123   BCD123   ABC123   BCD235

Since only two plates are identical, the first and the third, the correct answer is A.

1. PBV839	PVB839	PVB839	PVB839	1._____
2. WTX083	WTX083	WTX083	WTX083	2._____
3. B73609	D73906	BD7396	BD7906	3._____
4. AK7423	AK7423	AK1423	A81324	4._____
5. 583Y10	683Y10	583Y01	583Y10	5._____

Questions 6-10

DIRECTIONS: Questions 6 through 10 consist of groups of numbers and letters similar to those which might appear on license plates. Each group of numbers and letters will be called a license identification. Choose the license identification lettered A, B, C, or D that *EXACTLY* matches the license identification shown next to the question number.

SAMPLE
NY 1977
ABC-123

A. NY 1976   B. NY 1977   C. NY 1977   D. NY 1977
    ABC-123   ABC-132   CBA-123   ABC-123

The license identification given is NY 1977. The only choice
ABC-123.
that exactly matches it is the license identification next to the letter D. The correct answer is therefore D.

6.   NY 1976   6._____
                                       QLT-781

    A. NJ 1976   B. NY 1975   C. NY 1976   D. NY 1977
        QLT-781   QLT-781   QLT-781   QLT-781

7.   FLA 1977   7._____
                                       2-7LT58J

    A. FLA 1977   B. FLA 1977   C. FLA 1977   D. LA 1977
        2-7TL58J   2-7LTJ58   2-7LT58J   2-7LT58J

8.   NY 1975   8._____
                                       OQC383

    A. NY 1975   B. NY 1975   C. NY 1975   D. NY 1977
        OQC383   OQC833   QCQ383   OCQ383

9.   MASS 1977   9._____
                                       B-8DK02

    A. MISS 1977   B. MASS 1977   C. MASS 1976   D. MASS 1977
        B-8DK02   B-8DK02   B-8DK02   B-80KD2

10.   NY 1976   10._____
                                       ZV0586

    A. NY 1976   B. NY 1977   C. NY 1976   D. NY 1976
        2V0586   ZV0586   ZV0586   ZU0586

KEY (CORRECT ANSWERS)

1.	B		6.	C
2.	C		7.	C
3.	D		8.	A
4.	A		9.	B
5.	A		10.	C

TEST 6

DIRECTIONS: Assume that each of the capital letters in the table below represents the name of an employee enrolled in the city employees' retirement system. The number directly beneath the letter represents the agency for which the employee works, and the small letter directly beneath represents the code for the employee's account.

Name of Employee	L	O	T	Q	A	M	R	N	C
Agency	3	4	5	9	8	7	2	1	6
Account Code	r	f	b	i	d	t	g	e	n

In each of the following questions 1 through 3, the agency code numbers and the account code letters in Columns 2 and 3 should correspond to the capital letters in Column 1 and should be in the same consecutive order. For each question, look at each column carefully and mark your answer as follows:

If there are one or more errors *in Column 2 only* , mark your answer A.
If there are one or more errors *in Column 3 only,* mark your answer B.
If there are one or more errors in Column 2 and one or more errors in Column 3, mark your answer C.
If there are NO errors in either column, mark your answer D.
The following sample question is given to help you understand the procedure.

Column I	Column 2	Column 3
TQLMOC	583746	birtfn

In Column 2, the second agency code number (corresponding to letter Q) should be "9", not "8". Column 3 is coded correctly to Column 1. Since there is an error only in Column 2, the correct answer is A.

	Column 1	Column 2	Column 3	
1.	QLNRCA	931268	iregnd	1.____
2.	NRMOTC	127546	egftbn	2.____
3.	RCTALM	265837	gndbrt	3.____

KEY (CORRECT ANSWERS)

1. D
2. C
3. B

ARITHMETICAL REASONING
EXAMINATION SECTION
TEST 1

DIRECTIONS: Each question or incomplete statement is followed by several suggested answers or completions. Select the one that BEST answers the question or completes the statement. *PRINT THE LETTER OF THE CORRECT ANSWER IN THE SPACE AT THE RIGHT.*

1. At a certain city garage, there are 216 cars. Of these, 1/2 are assigned to Department P, 1/3 to Department Q, 1/9 to Department R, and the rest to Department S. How many cars are assigned to Department S?   1.____

   A.   9   B.   12   C.   18   D.   24

2. In August a car travels 572 miles; in September, 438 miles; in October, 898 miles; and in December it travels 609 miles.   2.____
   If the five month average from August through December was 673 miles traveled a month, then the number of miles traveled in November was

   A.   638   B.   706   C.   774   D.   848

3. Suppose the Units R, S, and T gave out a total of 1,715 parking tickets.   3.____
   If Unit R gave out twice as many tickets as Unit S, and Unit T gave out twice as many tickets as Unit R, the number of tickets given out by Unit S is

   A.   270   B.   255   C.   245   D.   225

4. A car travels at the average rate of 40 miles an hour on the highway.   4.____
   If it takes 5 hours to make a trip of 150 miles, 2/3 of which is on the highway and the rest on city streets, what was the AVERAGE rate of speed of the car on city streets?

   A.   20   B.   25   C.   30   D.   35

5. A motorist uses 27 gallons of gas on a trip of 351 miles. How many gallons of gas would he use if he took a trip of 624 miles under the same condition?   5.____

   A.   45   B.   46   C.   47   D.   48

6. If the taxi rate in the city is 35 for the first 1/5 of a mile and 5 for each additional 1/5 of a mile, how far did a passenger travel whose fare was 95¢?   6.____
   _____ miles.

   A.   2 1/5   B.   2 3/5   C.   3 2/5   D.   3 4/5

7. If you drove a car for three-quarters of an hour and kept it at a steady speed of 30 miles per hour for half an hour and a steady speed of 40 miles per hour the rest of the time, you would have traveled _____ miles.   7.____

   A.   20   B.   25   C.   30   D.   35

8. The length of curb available for the parking of cars on a certain street is 435 feet on the south side and 405 feet on the north side.
Assuming that the bumper-to-bumper length of the average car to be parked is 15 feet, the TOTAL number of cars that can be parked bumper-to-bumper on both sides of the street will be

   A.   56   B.   58   C.   60   D.   61

8.____

9. If the charges against a certain vehicle total $2,000 a year, and 7 1/2% of this is for repairs and maintenance, then the annual cost of repairs and maintenance for that vehicle is

   A. $50   B. $100   C. $150   D. $300

9.____

10. A 210 foot by 120 foot parking lot is reduced in size by construction of a 36 foot by 54 foot building at one of its corners.
The area left for parking is MOST NEARLY _____ square yards.

   A.   1,800   B.   2,600   C.   22,800   D.   23,300

10.____

11. A dispatcher works a total of 44 hours, spending 17 on Special Project A, 13 on Special Project B, and the rest on his usual duties.
The percentage of time he spends on the two special projects is MOST NEARLY

   A.   68%   B.   69%   C.   70%   D.   71%

11.____

12. A driver, dispatched from the garage at 8:15 A.M., arrived at his first destination 35 minutes later. He waited 50 minutes at this location before he could go on to his next destination. It took him one hour and 40 minutes traveling time to get to this second location. He then took an hour lunch period before driving back to the garage, a trip that took 45 minutes.
What time did the driver return to the garage?

   A.   12:25 P.M.   B.   12:45 P.M.
   C.   1:05 P.M.   D.   1:25 P.M.

12.____

13. Truck A has been driven 38,742.3 miles, Truck B has been driven 24,169.7 miles, Truck C has been driven 41,286.4 miles, Truck D has been driven 15,053.5 miles, and Truck E has been driven 8,407.0 miles.
The total mileage of these five trucks combined is MOST NEARLY _____ miles.

   A.   127,650   B.   127,660   C.   128,650   D.   128,660

13.____

14. Suppose that the trucks in a certain garage used a total of 86,314 gallons of gas in 1991 and 8,732 gallons less in 1992.
If they used a total of 72,483 gallons of gas in 1993, how much LESS gas was used in 1993 than in 1992?
_____ gallons.

   A.   5,099   B.   5,109   C.   5,199   D.   5,209

14.____

15. A driver averaged 17 miles for each gallon of gas used one week and 26 miles the next week.
If he used 38.9 gallons during the first week and 27.6 during the second, the TOTAL number of miles he drove in these two weeks was

   A.   1,266.3   B.   1,322.6   C.   1,378.9   D.   1,435.2

15.____

16. In Garage A, 87 drivers worked a total of 427 hours overtime. In Garage B, 53 drivers worked a total of 245 hours overtime.
Compared to the average overtime worked per man in Garage B, the average overtime worked per man in Garage A was MOST NEARLY _____ of an hour _____.

    A. 2/10; more   B. 2/10; less
    C. 3/10; more   D. 3/10; less

16.____

17. The scale on a map indicates that every 1 5/8 inches on the map represents 5 miles. If two locations are 13 inches apart on the map, what is the distance between them in miles?

    A. 30   B. 35   C. 40   D. 45

17.____

18. The number of yards in a mile is

    A. 5,280   B. 1,760   C. 880   D. 440

18.____

19. Add the following numbers: 17 1/2, 29 1/2, and 6 1/2. The CORRECT total is

    A. 32   B. 42   C. 53 1/2   D. 96 1/2

19.____

20. Add 1,516 and 3,497; then subtract 766.
The CORRECT answer is

    A. 2,731   B. 4,247   C. 5,357   D. 5,779

20.____

21. Add 39, 24, and 36. Then divide the total by 3.
The CORRECT answer is

    A. 23   B. 33   C. 96   D. 99

21.____

22. A certain paint can cover 310 square feet per gallon. The number of gallons of this paint required to paint 200 lines each 6 inches wide and 18 feet 6 inches long is MOST NEARLY

    A. 2   B. 4   C. 6   D. 8

22.____

23. A white paint that can cover 500 square feet of surface per gallon is used to paint the crosswalks at street intersections.
If the area at each intersection is equal to 300 square feet, the number of gallons required to paint 50 intersections is

    A. 10   B. 20   C. 30   D. 40

23.____

24. The dimension 45" expressed in feet is

    A. 3 1/3   B. 3 1/2   C. 3 3/4   D. 3 7/8

24.____

25. 85 percent of $5,250 is

    A. $3,463.50   B. $4,361.50
    C. $4,462.50   D. $4,666.50

25.____

KEY (CORRECT ANSWERS)

1.	B		11.	A
2.	D		12.	C
3.	C		13.	B
4.	A		14.	A
5.	D		15.	C
6.	B		16.	C
7.	B		17.	C
8.	A		18.	B
9.	C		19.	C
10.	B		20.	B

21. B
22. C
23. C
24. C
25. C

————

SOLUTIONS TO PROBLEMS

1. $(1 - 1/2 - 1/3 - 1/9)(216) = 12$ cars

2. Let x = miles traveled in November. Then, $(572+438+898+x+609)/5 = 673$. Solving, x = 848

3. Let 2x, x, 4x = number of tickets respectively issued by R, S, T. Then, $2x + x + 4x = 1715$. Solving, x = 245

4. Let x = speed on city streets. Then, $\dfrac{100}{40} + \dfrac{50}{x} = 5$ Simplifying, $100x + 2000 = 200x$. Solving, x = 20 mph.

5. $351 \div 27 = 13$ miles per gallon. Then, $624 \div 13 = 48$ gallons

6. Let x = number of miles. Then, $.35 + .25(x - 1/5) = .95$ Solving, x = 2 3/5

7. $(30x.50) + (40x.25) = 25$ miles

8. $(435+405)/15 = 56$ cars

9. Annual cost of repairs and maintenance = $(.075)(\$2000) = \$150$

10. Area left = $(210')(120') - (36')(54) = 23,256$ sq.ft., closest to 23,300
    sq.ft. $\approx 23,300 \div 9 \approx 2600$ sq.yds.

11. $(13+17)/44 = 68.\overline{18}\% \approx 68\%$

12. 8:15 AM + 35 min. + 50 min. + 1 hr. 40 min. + 1 hr. +45 min. = 8:15 AM + 4 hrs. 50 min. = 1:05 PM

13. $38,742.3 + 24,169.7 + 41,286.4 + 15,053.5 + 8407.0 = 127,658.9 \approx 127,660$ miles

14. $86,314 - 8732 - 72,483 = 5099$ gallons less

15. $(38.9)(17) + (27.6)(26) = 1378.9$ miles

16. Garage A: $427/87 \approx 4.9$ Garage B: $245/53 \approx 4.6$
    So, average overtime was 3/10 of an hour more in Garage A

17. $13 \div 1\,5/8 = 8$. Then, $(8X5) = 40$ miles

18. 1 mile = $5280 \div 3 = 1760$ yds.

19. $17\,1/2 + 29\,1/2 + 6\,1/2 = 53\,1/2$

20. $1516 + 3497 - 766 = 4247$

21. $(39+24+36) \div 3 = 99 \div 3 = 33$

22. $(200)(1/2')(18\,1/2') = 1850$ sq.ft. Then, $1850 \div 310 \approx 6$ gallons

23. $(50)(300$ sq.ft.$) = 15,000$ sq.ft. Then, $15,000 \div 500 = 30$ gallons

24. $45" = 45/12 = 3\,3/4$ ft.

25. $(\$5250)(.85) = \$4462.50$

TEST 2

DIRECTIONS: Each question or incomplete statement is followed by several suggested answers or completions. Select the one that BEST answers the question or completes the statement. *PRINT THE LETTER OF THE CORRECT ANSWER IN THE SPACE AT THE RIGHT.*

1. A vehicle which averages 14 1/2 miles to a gallon of gas uses a quart of oil for every 2 1/2 gallons of gas.
    If the vehicle traveled 19,952 miles in a year, its oil consumption for the year would be _____ quarts.

    A.   52   B.   56   C.   60   D.   64   1._____

2. Thirteen percent of all the vehicles in a certain garage are trucks.
    If there are 26 trucks, then the number of vehicles of other types in this garage is

    A.   174   B.   200   C.   260   D.   338   2._____

3.   Of 12 employees in a garage, four earn $35,000 a year, two earn $31,500 a year, one earns $45,500 a year, and the rest each earn $38,000 a year.
    The average yearly salary of these employees is CLOSEST to

    A. $35,500   B. $36,500   C. $37,500   D. $38,500   3._____

4. A garage bin used for storing supplies and parts measures 1 yard x 2 yards x 7 feet.
    The cubic volume of this bin is

    A.   5 1/3 cubic yards   B.   16 cubic feet
    C.   63 cubic feet   D.   126 cubic feet   4._____

5. A garage has a gas tank with a capacity of 1,300 gallons. If there are only 520 gallons of gas in the tank, then the tank is _____ full.

    A.   40%   B.   33 1/3%   C.   25%   D.   16 3/4%   5._____

6. Of a specially selected group of vehicles, 1/5 are 6 months old, 2/5 are 12 months old, and 2/5 are 15 months old.
    The average age of this group of vehicles is _____ months.

    A.   9   B.   10   C.   11   D.   12   6._____

7. A section of a garage used for parking vehicles measures 162 1/2' x 25 3/4'.
    If each vehicle to be parked in this section requires on the average 84 sq. ft. of parking space, the MAXIMUM number of vehicles that can be parked in this section is CLOSEST to

    A.   50   B.   45   C.   40   D.   35   7._____

8. Each of the 23 vehicles in a garage uses an average of 114 gallons of gas every 4 weeks.
    If the motor vehicle dispatcher is required to re-order gas when the gas tank in the garage shows no more than a one week supply, he MUST re-order when the gas tank shows _____ gallons.

    A.   655   B.   705   C.   830   D.   960   8._____

9. An employee's annual salary is $45,800. His total annual deductions are 22% for with-   9.____
holding tax, 8% for pension and social security, and $1,820 for health insurance. The
take-home pay that this employee would get on the check he receives every other week
is MOST NEARLY

    A. $577.10   B. $845.00   C. $1,154.20   D. $1,220.40

10. The list price of truck A is $12,500 and that of truck B is $12,000.   10.____
If the discount on truck A is 20% and the discount on truck B is 10%, how much
cheaper would it be to buy truck A instead of truck B?

    A. $800   B. $450   C. $400   D.   No cheaper

11. There are three garages located in a single block. Garage A has 3/4 of the capacity of   11.____
garage B and 2/3 of the capacity of garage C.
If 88 cars can be parked in garage B, the TOTAL number of cars that can be parked in
all of the three garages is

    A.   186   B.   205   C.   238   D.   253

12. The city purchases 5 vehicles costing $6,000 each, 3 vehicles costing $8,000 each, and   12.____
2 vehicles costing $13,000 each.
The TOTAL cost of these vehicles is

    A. $67,000   B. $26,000   C. $80,000   D. $84,000

13. A car that averages 15 miles per gallon of gas is driven 135 miles. The gas tank is then   13.____
filled to capacity by pumping in 12 gallons of gas.
If the gas tank holds 18 gallons when full, the amount of gas in the tank at the beginning of the 135 mile trip must have been _____ gallons.

    A.   6   B.   9   C.   12   D.   15

14. Suppose that a car ran a total of 9,888 miles in a four-month period from September   14.____
through December, inclusive. It used 234 gallons of gas in September, 203 gallons in
October, 191 gallons in November, and 196 gallons in December.
The AVERAGE number of miles it traveled per gallon of gasoline was

    A.   10   B.   11   C.   12   D.   12 1/2

15. A government agency has a policy of replacing 1/3 of its vehicles each year. Of the 20   15.____
vehicles the agency is requesting in the budget, 95% are replacements.
If the request is granted, the TOTAL number of vehicles in the agency will be

    A.   19   B.   27   C.   58   D.   61

16. Car A averaged 21 miles to a gallon of gas. Car B averaged 18 miles to a gallon of gas.   16.____
Each car used 14 gallons of gas.
How many miles more did car A travel than car B?

    A.   42   B.   39   C.   28   D.   14

17. A garage has a gas tank with a capacity of 500 gallons. During the week, 210 gallons   17.____
were used and 340 gallons were delivered at the end of the week to fill the tank. How
many gallons of gas were in the tank at the beginning of the week?

    A.   160   B.   210   C.   340   D.   370

18. The list price of vehicle A is $4,200 and that of vehicle B is $3,800. The city can get a dis-   18.____
count of 20% of the list price on vehicle A and 10% of the list price on vehicle B.
How much cheaper can the city buy vehicle A than vehicle B?

   A. $20   B. $60   C. $200   D. $600

19. In a certain bureau, there are 4 employees who each earn $250 a week, 12 employees   19.____
who each earn $300 a week , and 2 employees who each earn $350 a week.
The weekly payroll for all these employees is

   A. $4,900   B. $5,100   C. $5,300   D. $5,500

20. If the average passenger car needs 120 square feet of parking space, the LARGEST   20.____
number of such cars that could be parked in a garage with a usable floor area that measures 70 feet by 100 feet is

   A.   52   B.   54   C.   56   D.   58

21. On a certain bridge, the toll for a motorcycle is 5/7 the toll for a passenger car and 1/3 the   21.____
toll for a truck. If the toll for a passenger car is $1.75 then the toll for a truck on this bridge
is

   A. $2,50   B. $3.75   C. $5.00   D. $6.25

22. If a car is traveling on a highway at a steady speed of 35 miles an hour, how many miles   22.____
will it go in a period of 24 minutes?

   A.   13   B.   14   C.   15   D.   16

23. An employee's monthly salary is $7,625.   23.____
If he receives a 5.4% salary increase, his new monthly salary will be

   A. $7,992.50   B. $8,036.75   C. $8,147.25   D. $8,169.00

24. Of the 60 drivers assigned to a garage, 1/6 of them live in County A, 1/4 of them live in   24.____
County B, 1/5 of them live in County C, and the rest live in County D.
How many of the drivers live in County D?

   A.   22   B.   23   C.   24   D.   25

25. Driver Green travels 33 miles along express highways at an average speed of 44 miles   25.____
an hour to get to his destination. Driver Smith travels 28 miles through traffic at an average speed of 21 miles an hour to get to the same destination.
If Mr. Smith starts his trip a half hour before Mr. Green, he will reach the destination
_____ Mr. Green.

   A.   5 minutes before   B.   at the same time as
   C.   5 minutes after   D.   10 minutes after

KEY (CORRECT ANSWERS)

1.	D		11.	D
2.	A		12.	C
3.	B		13.	D
4.	D		14.	C
5.	A		15.	C
6.	D		16.	A
7.	A		17.	D
8.	A		18.	B
9.	C		19.	C
10.	A		20.	D

21.	B
22.	B
23.	B
24.	B
25.	C

———————

SOLUTIONS TO PROBLEMS

1. 19,952 ÷ 14 1/2 = 1376 gallons of gas. Then, 1376 ÷ 21 1/2 = 64 quarts of oil

2. 26 ÷ .13 = 200 vehicles, including the trucks. The number of non-trucks = 200 - 26 = 174

3. [(4)($35,000)+(2)($31,500)+(1)($45,500)+(5)($38,000)] ÷ 12 = $36,541.67, closest to $36,500

4. (3 ft)(6 ft)(7 ft) = 126 cu.ft.

5. 520 ÷ 1300 = 40% full

6. [(1)(6)+(2)(12)+(2)(15)] ÷ 5 = 12 mos.

7. (162 1/2)(25 3/4) ÷ 84 ≈ 49.8, closest to 50 vehicles

8. 114 ÷ 44 = 28.5 . Then, (28.5)(23) ≈ 655 gallons

9. $45,800 - (.22)($45,800) - (.085)($45,800) - $1820 = $30,011
   Amount for every other week = $30,011 ÷ 26 ≈ $1154.20

10. ($12,500)(.80) - ($12,000)(.90) = -$800, so truck A is $800 cheaper than truck B.

11. Garage A holds (3/4)(88) =66 cars and garage C holds 66 ÷ 2/3 = 99 cars. Thus, all 3 garages hold 66 + 88 + 99 = 253 cars

12. Total cost = (5)($6000) + (3)($8000) + (2)($13,000) = $80,000

13. Let x = gallons of gas in the tank at the beginning.

    Then, x - 135/15 + 12 = 18. Solving, x = 15

14. Average = 9888 ÷ (234+203+191+196) = 12 miles per gallon

15. (20)(.95) = 19 replacements. Total number of vehicles = (19)(3) + 1 = 58

16. (21)(14) - (18)(14) = 42 miles

17. Let x = number of gallons in the tank at the beginning of the week. Then, x - 210 + 340 = 500. Solving, x = 370

18. ($3800)(.90) - ($4200)(.80) = $60. So, vehicle A is $60 cheaper than vehicle B.

19. (4)($250) + (12)($300) + (2)($350) = $5300

20. (70)(100) ÷ 120 = 58 .$\overline{3}$ so 58 cars is the maximum.

21. (5/7)($1.75) = $1.25 = toll for a motorcycle.Then, the toll for a truck = 1.25 ÷ 1/3 = $ 3.75

22. (35)(24/60) = 14 miles

23. ($7625)(1.054) = $8036.75

24. 60(1 - 1/6 - 1/4 - 1/5) = 23 drivers

25. Green requires 33/44 = 3/4hrs., whereas Smith requires 28/21 = 1 1/3 hr. Since Smith began 1/2 hr. sooner, he will reach his destination 1 1/3 - 1/2 - 3/4 = 1/12 = 5 min. after Green.

———

TEST 3

DIRECTIONS: Each question or incomplete statement is followed by several suggested answers or completions. Select the one that BEST answers the question or completes the statement. *PRINT THE LETTER OF THE CORRECT ANSWER IN THE SPACE AT THE RIGHT.*

1. Thirty miles per hour is equivalent to _____ feet per second.   1._____

   A.   30   B.   44   C.   60   D.   80

2. A driver whose car is parked for 8 hours in an off-street facility where the rate is 50 cents   2._____
   an hour for the first 5 hours and 75 cents an hour thereafter would pay

   A. $6.00   B. $5.75   C. $4.75   D. $4.00

3. An agent has written out 29 summonses for moving violations, 13 summonses for park-   3._____
   ing violations, and 3 summonses for other violations.
   The TOTAL number of summonses he has written out is

   A.   36   B.   42   C.   43   D.   45

4. A driver complains about being ticketed for parking too near a fire hydrant. He insists that   4._____
   his car is *at least 8 yards from the hydrant.*
   If he is right, how far away from the hydrant is his car, in terms of feet rather than
   yards?

   A.   16   B.   24   C.   30   D.   80

5. At the intersection of an avenue and a cross street, the traffic lights have been set so that   5._____
   traffic on the avenue has a green light for 55 seconds followed by a yellow light for 5 seconds, then traffic on the cross street has a green light for 25 seconds followed by a yellow
   light for 5 seconds.
   How long is a complete cycle of lights at this intersection, that is, how much time must
   pass from the moment the light turns from red to green until the moment the light will
   turn from red to green again?
   _____ seconds.

   A.   60   B.   70   C.   80   D.   90

6. An agent has jotted down the following notes on one day's work: 6._____
   8:00-11:30   On duty at intersection as assigned
   11:30 - 12:00   Off duty - lunch
   12:00-2:00   On duty - attending assigned training session
   2:00-4:00   On duty at intersection - replacement came late
   How many on-duty hours do this agent's notes show for this particular day?

   A.   4   B.   7   C.   7 1/2   D.   8

7. If a traffic jam of 78 vehicles occurs at the intersection you are controlling, and if one car   7._____
   can pass through the intersection every 10 seconds, how long will it take to clear these
   78 vehicles out of the intersection?
   _____ minutes.

   A.   5.2   B.   7.8   C.   13.0   D.   15.7

8. An agent issued the following summonses in one day: 12 summonses at $25 each, 5 summonses at $15 each, and 3 summonses at $10 each.
What is the TOTAL amount of the fines for the summonses he gave out on that day?

   A. $305   B. $315   C. $405   D. $485   8._____

9. If the difference in elevation between two intersections 300 feet apart is 6 feet, the grade along the street is

   A. 2%   B. 2   C. 0.002   D. 6%   9._____

10. If on a highway a car passes a given point every 5 seconds, the number of cars per hour passing the given point on the highway is

    A. 360   B. 480   C. 600   D. 720   10._____

11. The cost of concrete paving for a strip of driveway 50 feet long, 10 feet wide, and 6 inches deep, if concrete in place costs $30 per cubic yard, is, in dollars, MOST NEARLY
(27 cubic feet = 1 cubic yard)

    A. 278   B. 318   C. 329   D. 380   11._____

12. The sketch at the right shows a right triangular island at the intersection of three streets on which is installed traffic signals A and B. Traffic conditions have increased and require that an additional traffic light be installed at point C. Electric power for signal C is to be taken from the junction box located at the base of post A and extended to C, as shown by the broken line.
With the distances given as shown, the length of conduit, in feet, required to extend power from A to C is MOST NEARLY

    A. 44   B. 60   C. 83   D. 75   12._____

13. The volume of traffic at a certain location increased from 1,000 to 1,500 vehicles per hour.
The percentage increase of traffic is MOST NEARLY

    A. 33%   B. 50%   C. 60%   D. 40%   13._____

14. During a certain three-month period, the bureau of enforcement issued 239,788 summonses. Of these, 37,900 were issued between the hours of 12 Noon and 1 P.M.; 33,350 were issued between 1 P.M. and 2 P.M.; and 23,334 were issued between 2 P.M. and 3 P.M.
What percentage of the total number of summonses issued during this three-month period was issued between 1 P.M. and 3 P.M.?

    A. 22%   B. 24%   C. 26%   D. 28%   14._____

15. A city has 51,489 parking meters. Thirteen percent of them require repairs.
Therefore, the number of meters requiring repairs is MOST NEARLY

    A. 6,690   B. 6,695   C. 6,700   D. 6,705   15._____

16. The following sums of money were collected from parking meters in an eight-week period: $15,298, $14,248, $16,873, $18,137, $18,256, $19,342, $18,437, and $15,432. Therefore, the total amount collected from these meters for this eight-week period was MOST NEARLY

16.____

    A. $135,150   B. $135,985   C. $136,025   D. $136,543

17. There were 68,937 meters in operation at the end of December. Exactly one year later, there were 102,331 meters in operation.
Therefore, the increase in the number of meters in operation is MOST NEARLY

17.____

    A. 34,400   B. 33,900   C. 33,400   D. 32,900

18. In a certain city, there are 24,482 parking meters. Of these meters, 3/8 are in Zone A. Therefore, the number of meters in Zone A is MOST NEARLY

18.____

    A. 3,060   B. 8,160   C. 9,180   D. 12,240

19. It costs $55,525 to service 9,995 parking meters.
Therefore, the cost of servicing one meter is MOST NEARLY

19.____

    A. $2.50   B. $3.50   C. $4.50   D. $5.50

20. Of 165 parking meters, 0.14 of the total are out of order.
Therefore, the number of these parking meters out of order is MOST NEARLY

20.____

    A. 83   B. 23   C. 8   D. 2.31

21. Suppose that a city block on a parking meter collector's route is 260 feet wide by 780 feet long.
Therefore, the area of this block, in square feet, is MOST NEARLY

21.____

    A. 1,040   B. 2,080   C. 104,000   D. 203,000

22. The base of a container for coin boxes measures 2 feet by 3 feet. The base of the coin boxes measures 2 inches by 3 inches.
The GREATEST number of coin boxes that will fit into the container in a single layer is

22.____

    A. 36   B. 72   C. 100   D. 144

23. The total collected from parking meters in city A for a 12-month period was $701,790. Therefore, the average collected per month for this 12-month period was MOST NEARLY

23.____

    A. $58,481   B. $58,483   C. $58,485   D. $8,421,480

24. It costs $158.46 each week to maintain the parking meters in a certain city.
Therefore, to maintain these meters for 372 weeks would cost MOST NEARLY

24.____

    A. $58,950   B. $58,975   C. $59,000   D. $59,025

25. Two attendants earn $6,240 and $6,220 per annum, respectively, exclusive of a bonus of $2,640 per annum.
If both have a pension deduction of 20%, the difference in the pension deduction of the two attendants on a semimonthly basis is

25.____

    A. $1.50   B. $.50   C. $1.00   D. $.17

KEY (CORRECT ANSWERS)

1.	B		11.	A
2.	C		12.	B
3.	D		13.	B
4.	B		14.	B
5.	D		15.	B
6.	C		16.	C
7.	C		17.	C
8.	C		18.	C
9.	A		19.	D
10.	D		20.	B

21. D
22. D
23. B
24. A
25. D

—————

SOLUTIONS TO PROBLEMS

1. Since 60 mi/hr = 88 ft/sec, 30 mi/hr = 44 ft/sec

2. ($.50)(5) + ($.75)(3) = $4.75

3. 29 + 13 + 3 = 45 summonses

4. (8)(3) = 24 feet

5. One cycle = 55 + 5 + 25 + 5 = 90 seconds

6. 3 1/2 + 2 + 2 = 7 1/2 hrs. on duty

7. (78)(10) = 780 sec. = 13 min.

8. (12)($25) + (5)($15) + (3)($10) = $405

9. $\dfrac{6}{300}$ = .02 = 2% grade

10. 60 ÷ 5 = 12 per min. Then, (12)(60) = 720 cars per hr.

11. ($30)(50)(10)(1/2) ÷ 27 ≈ $278

12. Distance from A to C = $\sqrt{30^2 + 53^2} = \sqrt{3709} \approx 60$ ft.

13. $\dfrac{500}{1000}$ = 50% increase

14. (33,350+23,334) ÷ 239,788 = 56,684 ÷ 239,788 ≈ 24%

15. (51,489)(.13) = 6693.57, closest to 6695

16. $15,298 + $14,248 + $16,873 + $18,137 + $18,256 + $19,342 + $18,437 + $15,432 = $136,023, closest to $136,025

17. 102,331 - 68,937 = 33,394, closest to 33,400

18. (3/8)(24,482) = 9180.75, nearest to 9180

19. $55,525 ÷ 9995 ≈ $5.56, closest to $5.50

20. (.14)(165) = 23.1 ≈ 23

21. (260)(780) = 202,800 sq.ft. ≈ 203,000 sq.ft.

22. [(2')(3')] ÷ [(2/12')(3/12')] = 144 coin boxes maximum

23. $701,790 ÷ 12 = $58,483

24. $158.46)(372) = $58,947.12 ≈ $58,950

25. ($6240-$6220)(.20) = $4 per year. This equates to $4 ÷ 24 ≈ 17 cents per half-month.

THE ENGLISH AND METRIC SYSTEMS OF MEASUREMENT

TABLE OF CONTENTS

THE ENGLISH AND METRIC SYSTEMS OF MEASUREMENT

A. The English System. Tables of weights and measures have been established by law and custom. These units of measurement are concrete numbers commonly referred to as *denominate numbers*.

1. LINEAR (LINE OR LONG) MEASURE

Used in measuring distances and lengths, widths, or thicknesses.

12 inches (in.)	= 1 foot (ft.)
3 feet	= 1 yard (yd.)
5 1/2 yards, or 16 1/2 feet	= 1 rod (rd.)
40 rods	= 1 furlong (fur.).
8 furlongs, or 320 rods	= 1 mile (mi.)

The unit of length is the yard.
1 hand = 4 inches (used in measuring the height of horses).
1 fathom (marine measure) = 6 feet (used in measuring depths at sea).
1 knot = 1.152 1/2 miles (nautical or geographical mile).
1 league =3 knots (3 X 1.15 miles).

2. SQUARE (SURFACE) MEASURE

Used in measuring areas of surfaces.

144 square inches (sq. in.)	= 1 square foot (sq. ft.)
9 square feet	= 1 square yard (sq. yd.)
30 1/4 square yards	= 1 square rod (sq. rd.)
160 square rods	= 1 acre (A.)
640 acres	= 1 square mile (sq. mi.)

The unit in measuring land is the acre, except for city lots.
A square, used in roofing, is 100 square feet.
The unit in measuring other surfaces is the square yard.

3. CUBIC MEASURE

Used in measuring the volume of a body or a solid as well as the contents or capacity of hollow bodies.

1,728 cubic inches (cu. in.)	= 1 cubic foot (cu. ft.)
27 cubic feet	= 1 cubic yard (cu. yd.)
231 cubic inches	= 1 gallon (gal.)
24 3/4 cubic feet	= 1 perch (P.)
128 cubic feet	= 1 cord (cd.)
1 cubic foot	= 7 1/2 gallons

1 cubic yard of earth = 1 load.
A cord of wood (128 cubic feet) is a pile 8 feet long, 4 feet wide, and 4 feet high.
1 cubic foot of water weighs 62 1/2 pounds (avoirdupois).

4. CIRCULAR OR ANGULAR MEASURE

Used in measuring angles or areas of circles.

60 seconds (")	= 1 minute (')	30 degrees = 1 sign (1/12 of a circle)	
60 minutes	= 1 degree (°)	60 degrees = 1 sextant (1/6 of a circle)	
360 degrees	= 1 circle (cir.)	90 degrees = 1 quadrant (1/4 of a circle)	

A 90° angle is a right angle.

5. LIQUID MEASURE

Used in measuring the liquid capacity of vessels or containers of all liquids except medicine.

4 gills (gi.)	= 1 pint (pt.)	63 gallons	= 1 hogshead (hhd.)
2 pints	= 1 quart (qt.)	2 barrels	= 1 hogshead
4 quarts	= 1 gallon (gal.)	7 1/2 gallons	= 1 cubic foot
31 1/2 gallons	= 1 barrel (bbl.)		

The unit of liquid measure is the United States gallon of 231 cubic inches.
1 gallon of water weighs 8 1/3 pounds (avoirdupois).

6. DRY MEASURE

Used in measuring the volume of the contents of containers of solids, such as produce, seed, fruits, etc., that are not sold by weight.

2 pints (pt.)	= 1 quart (qt.)	4 pecks = 1 bushel (bu.)	
8 quarts	= 1 peck (pk.)	2 3/4 bushels = 1 barrel	

7. AVOIRDUPOIS WEIGHT

Used in weighing heavy, coarse articles, such as coal, iron, grain, hay, etc.

16 ounces (oz.)	= 1 pound (lb.)
100 pounds	= 1 hundredweight (cwt.)
20 hundredweights	= 1 ton (T.)
2,000 pounds	= 1 ton
2,240 pounds	= 1 long or gross ton
7,000 grains (gr.)	= 1 pound avoirdupois

The United States Government uses the long ton of 2,240 pounds in fixing the duty on merchandise that is taxed by the ton.
Coal and iron sold at the mine are also weighed by the long ton.

8. TROY WEIGHT

Used in weighing precious minerals, and by the United States Government in weighing coins.

24 grains	= 1 pennyweight (pwt.)
20 pennyweights	= 1 ounce
12 ounces	= 1 pound
240 pennyweights	= 1 pound
5,760 grains	= 1 pound troy
3,168 grains	= 1 carat

The unit of weight in the United States is the troy pound.

Pure gold is 24 carats fine. Gold marked 14 carats is 14/24, by weight, pure gold and 10/24, by weight, alloy.

9. APOTHECARIES' DRY WEIGHT AND LIQUID MEASURE

Used by druggists and physicians in weighing and measuring drugs and chemicals, and in compounding dry and liquid medicines.

APOTHECARIES' DRY WEIGHT

20 grains	= 1 scruple (sc.)
3 scruples	= 1 dram (dr.)
8 drams	= 1 ounce (oz.)
12 ounces	= 1 pound (lb.)

APOTHECARIES' FLUID MEASURE

60 minims (m.)	= 1 fluid drachm, or dram (f3)
8 fluid drachms	= 1 fluid ounce (f3)
16 fluid ounces	= 1 pint (O.)
8 pints	= 1 gallon (Cong.)

Avoirdupois weight is used when drugs and chemicals are bought and sold wholesale.

10. TIME TABLE

60 seconds (sec.)	= 1 minute (min.)	52 weeks	= 1 year (yr.)
60 minutes	= 1 hour (hr.)	12 months	= 1 year
24 hours	= 1 day (da.)	365 days	= 1 year*
7 days	=1 week (wk.)	100 years	= 1 century (C.)
30 days	=1 month (mo.)*		

* January, 31 days; February, 28 days (29 days in February in a leap year of 366 days); March, 31 days; April, 30 days; May, 31 days; June, 30 days; July, 31 days; August, 31 days; September, 30 days; October, 31 days; November, 30 days; December, 31 days.

4

11. COUNTING TABLE

20 units	= 1 score
12 units	= 1 dozen
12 dozen	= 1 gross (gro.)
12 gross	= 1 great gross (gr. gro.)

12. PAPER MEASURE

24	sheets	= 1 quire (qr.)
20	quires	= 1 ream (rm.)
2	reams	= 1 bundle (bdl.)
5	bundles	= 1 bale (bl.)

13. MEASURES OF VALUE

United States Money

10 mills	= 1 cent
10 cents	= 1 dime
10 dimes	= 1 dollar
10 dollars	= 1 eagle

The unit of measure is the dollar.

English Money

4	farthings (far.)	= 1 penny (d)
12	pence	= 1 shilling (s.)
20	shillings	= 1 pound sterling ()

The unit of measure is the pound sterling.

French Money

10 millimes (m.)	= 1 centime (c.)
10 centimes	= 1 decime (dc.)
10 decimes	= 1 franc (F.)

The unit of measure is the franc.

German Money

100 pfennig (pf.)	= 1 mark

The unit of measure is the mark.

14. COMMODITY WEIGHTS

Beef, barrel	200	lbs.	Nails, keg	100	lbs.
Butter, firkin	56	lbs.	Pork, barrel	200	lbs.
Flour, barrel	196	lbs.	Salt, barrel	280	lbs.

15. BUSHEL WEIGHTS

The following weights are used in a bushel in most of the states:

Barley	48 lbs.	Corn (shelled)	56 lbs.	Potatoes	60 lbs.
Beans	60 lbs.	Corn meal	48 lbs.	Rye	56 lbs.
Buckwheat	48 lbs.	Oats	32 lbs.	Sweet potatoes	54 lbs.
Clover seed	60 lbs.	Onions	57 lbs.	Timothy seed	45 lbs.
Corn (ear)	70 lbs.	Peas	60 lbs.	Wheat	60 lbs.

B. The Metric System. The metric system of weights and measures is a decimal system. The three principal units are

1. The meter, which is the unit of length.
2. The liter, which is the unit of capacity.
3. The gram, which is the unit of weight or mass.

The basic unit of the metric system is the meter, upon which the other units are based. The length of the meter, which is 39.37 inches, was originally determined by taking one ten-millionth of the distance from the equator to the pole.

96

I. METRIC TABLES
1. LINEAR MEASURE

10 millimeters (mm.)	= 1 centimeter (cm.)
10 centimeters	= 1 decimeter (dm.)
10 decimeters	= 1 meter (m.)
10 meters	= 1 decameter (Dm.)
10 decameters	= 1 hectometer (Hm.)
10 hectometers	= 1 kilometer (Km.)
10 kilometers	= 1 myriameter (Mm.)

The unit of measures of length is the meter.

2. SQUARE MEASURE

100 square millimeters (sq. mm.)	= 1 square centimeter (sq. cm.)
100 square centimeters	= 1 square decimeter (sq. dm.)
100 square decimeters	= 1 square meter (sq. m.)
100 square meters	= 1 square decameter (sq. Dm.)
100 square decameters	= 1 square hectometer (sq. Hm.)
100 square hectometers	= 1 square kilometer (sq. Km.)

The unit of square measures is the square meter.

3. CUBIC MEASURE

1,000 cubic millimeters (cu. mm.)	= 1 cubic centimeter (cu. cm.)
1,000 cubic centimeters	= 1 cubic decimeter (cu. dm.)
1,000 cubic decimeters	= 1 cubic meter (cu. m.)
1,000 cubic meters	= 1 cubic decameter (cu. Dm.)
1,000 cubic decameters	= 1 cubic hectometer (cu. Hm.)
1,000 cubic hectometers	= 1 cubic kilometer (cu. Km.)

The unit of measures of volume is the cubic meter.

4. LIQUID AND DRY MEASURE

10 milliliters (ml.)	= 1 centiliter (cl.)	10 liters	= 1 decaliter (Dl.)
10 centiliters	= 1 deciliter (dl.)	10 decaliters	= 1 hectoliter (Hl.)
10 deciliters	= 1 liter (1.)	10 hectoliters	= 1 kiloliter (Kl)

The unit of capacity for liquids and solids is the liter.

5. WEIGHT TABLE

10 milligrams (mg.)	= 1 centigram (eg.)
10 centigrams	= 1 decigram (dg.)
10 decigrams	= 1 gram (g.)
10 grams	= 1 decagram (Dg.)
10 decagrams	= 1 hectogram (Hg.)
10 hectograms	= 1 kilogram (Kg.)
10 kilograms	= 1 myriagram (Mg.)
10 myriagrams	= 1 quintal (Q.)
10 quintals	= 1 tonneau (T.)

The unit of weight is the gram.

II. METRIC AND ENGLISH EQUIVALENTS
1. LINEAR-MEASURE EQUIVALENTS

1 in. = 2.54 cm.	1 cm. = .3937 in.
1 ft. = .3048 m.	1 dm. = .328 ft.
1 yd. = .9144 m.	1m. = 1.0936 yds.
1 rd. = 5.029 m.	1 Dm. = 1.9884 rds.
1 mi. = 1,6093 Km.	1Km. = .6214 mi.

2. SQUARE-MEASURE EQUIVALENTS

1 sq. in. = 6.452 sq. cm.	1 sq. cm. = .155 sq. in.
1 sq. ft. = .0929 sq. m.	1 sq. dm. = .1076 sq.ft.
1 sq. yd. = .8361 sq. m.	1 sq. m. = 1.196 sq. yds.
1 sq. rd. = 25.293 sq. m.	1 a. = 3.954 sq. rds.
1A. = 40.47 a. (ares)	1 ha. = 2.471 A.
1 sq. mi. = 259 ha. (hectares	1 sq. Km. = .3861 sq. mi.

3. CUBIC-MEASURE EQUIVALENTS

1 cu. in. = 16.387 cu. cm.	1 cu. cm. = .061 cu. in.
1 cu. ft. = 28.317 cu. dm.	1 cu. dm. = .0353 cu. ft.
1 cu. yd. = .7646 cu. m.	1 cu. m. = 1.308 cu. yds.
1 cd. = 3.624 st. (steres)	1 st. = .2759 cd.

4. LIQUID- AND DRY-MEASURE EQUIVALENTS

1 dry qt. = 1.1011.	1l. = .908 dry qt.
1 liquid qt. = .94631.	1l. = 1.0567 liquid qt.
1 liquid gal. = .3785 Di.	1Dl. = 2.6417 liquid gal.
1 pk. .881 Dl.	1Dl. = 1.135 pk.
1 bu. .3524 Hl.	1Hl. = 2.8377 bu.

5. WEIGHT-MEASURE EQUIVALENTS

1 qt. Troy = .0648 g.	1 g. = 15.432 gr. Troy
1 oz. Troy = 31. 104 g.	1 g. = .03215 oz. Troy
1 oz. Avoir. = 28.35 g.	1 g. = .03527 oz. Avoir.
1 lb. Troy = .3732 kg.	1 kg. = 2.679 lbs. Troy
1 lb. Avoir. = .4536 kg.	1 kg. = 2.2046 lbs. Avoir.
1 T. (short) = .9072 1.	1 t. = 1.1023 T. (short)

III. THE RELATIONSHIP OF AMERICAN AND METRIC UNITS

Pounds (avoirdupois)	X	.454	= Kilograms
Pounds (avoirdupois)	X	453.592	= Grams
Grams	X	.035	= Ounces
Ounces	X	28.35	= Grams
Kilograms	X	2.205	= Pounds
Grams	X	.002205	= Pounds
Quarts (liquid)	X	.946	= Liters
Quarts (liquid)	X	946.333	= Milliliters
Liters	X	1.057	= Quarts
Liters	X	1000.	= Milliliters
Milliliters	X	.001057	= Quarts

TABLES AND FORMULAS

A. TABLES

TABLES OF WEIGHTS AND MEASURES

LINEAR MEASURE OR MEASURES OF LENGTH

12 inches (in.)	= 1 foot (ft.)
3 feet	= 1 yard (yd.)
5.5 yards	= 1 rod (rd.)
320 rods	= 1 mile (mi.)

A mile = 320 rd. = 1760 yd. = 5280 ft. = 1.61 kilometers

SQUARE MEASURES OR MEASURES OF SURFACE

144 Square inches (sq. in.)	= 1 square foot (sq. ft.)
9 square feet	= 1 square yard (sq. yd.)
30.25 square yards	= 1 square rod (sq. rd.)
160 square rods	= 1 acre (A.)
640 acres	= 1 square mile (sq. mi.)

An acre = 160 sq. rd. = 4840 sq. yd. = 43,560 sq. ft.

CUBIC MEASURE OR MEASURES OF VOLUME

1728 cubic inches (cu. in.)	= 1 cubic foot (cu. ft.)
27 cubic feet	= 1 cubic yard (cu. yd.)
128 cubic feet	= 1 cord of wood of 4-ft. length

IMPORTANT VOLUME EQUIVALENTS

1 cubic foot	= 7.5 gallons (gal.)
1 cubic foot of water	= 62.5 pounds (lb.)
1 cubic foot	= 0.8 bushel (bu.)
1 gallon	= 231 cubic inches (cu. in.)
1 gallon of water	= 8 1/3 pounds (lb.)
1 cubic foot of ice	= 56 1/4 pounds (lb.)

MEASURES OF WEIGHT

16 ounces (oz)	= 1 pound (lb.)
100 pounds	= 1 hundredweight (cwt.)
2000 pounds	= 1 ton (T.)
2240 pounds	= 1 long ton

LIQUID MEASURES

4 gills (gi.)	= 1 pint (pt.)
16 fluid oz.	= 1 pint
2 pints	= 1 quart (qt.)
4 quarts	= 1 gallon (gal.)
31.5 gallons	= 1 barrel (bbl.)

DRY MEASURES

2 pints (pt.)	= 1 quart (qt.)
8 quarts	= 1 peck (pk.)
4 pecks	= 1 bushel (bu. -)
2 1/2 bushels	= 1 barrel (bbl.)

MEASURES CONVENIENT FOR PRACTICAL ESTIMATES

1 ton hard coal	= 35 cubic feet
1 bu. shelled corn or rye	= 56 lb.)
1 bu. corn in ear	= 70 lb.)
1 bu. oats	= 32 lb.) Legal weights vary
1 bu. wheat or potatoes	= 60 lb.) in different state
1 bu. apples or peaches	= 48 lb.)

MEASURES OF TIME

60 seconds (sec.)	= 1 minute (min.)
60 minutes	= 1 hour (hr.)
24 hours	= 1 day (da.)
7 days	= 1 week (wk.)
30 days (approx.)	= 1 month (mo.)
4 weeks (approx.)	= 1 month
12 months	= 1 year (yr.)
365 days	= 1 year
366 days	= 1 leap year
10 years	= 1 decade
100 years	= 1 century

UNITS OF COUNTING

12 units	= 1 dozen (doz.)
12 dozen	= 1 gross (gr.)
144 units	= 1 gross
20 units	= 1 score
24 sheets (of paper)	= 1 quire
20 quires	= 1 ream

MEASURES OF ANGLES AND ARCS

60 seconds (")	= 1 minute (')
60 minutes	= 1 degree (°)
360 degrees	= 1 circumference

TABLES OF ACCURATE METRIC EQUIVALENTS

LENGTH

1 inch	= 2.540 centimeters	1 millimeter	= .03937 inch
1 foot	= .3048 meter	1 centimeter	= .3937 inch
1 yard	= .9144 meter	1 meter	= 39.37 inches
		1 meter	= 3.281 feet
1 rod =	= 5.029	1 meter	= 1.094 yards
1 mile =	1.609 kilometers	1 kilometer	= .6214 mile

AREA

1 sq. inch	= 6.452 sq. cm.	1 sq. millimeter	= .00155 sq. in.
1 sq. foot	= .0929 sq. meter	1 sq. centimeter	= .1550 sq. in.
1 sq. yard	= .84 sq/ meter	1 sq. meter	= 1. 196 sq. yd.
1 sq. roc.	= 25.29 sq. meters	1 sq. kilometer	= . 3861 sq. mi.
1 sq. mile	= 2.589 sq. kilom.	1 hectare	= 2.471 acres
1 acre	= .4047 hectare		

VOLUME AND CAPACITY

1 cu. in.	= 16.3872 cu. centimeters	1 cu. centimeter	= .06102 cu. in.
1 cu. ft.	= .02832 cu. meter	1 cubic meter	= 1.308 cu. yd.
1 cu. yd.	= .7646 cu. meter	1 milliliter	= .03381 liq. oz.
1 liquid qt.	= .9464 liter	1 liter	=1.057 liq. qt.
1 liquid gal.	= 3.785 liters	1 liter	= .9081 dry qt.
1 dry qt,	= 1.101 liters	1 hektoliter	= 2.838 bushels
1 peck	= 8.810 liters	1 dekaliter	=1.135 pecks
1 bushel	= .3524 hektoliter	1 dekaliter	= 2.642 liq. gal.

WEIGHT

1 grain	= .0648 gram	1 gram	= 15.43 grains (troy)
1 oz. (avoir)	= 28.35 grams	1 gram	= .03215 oz. (troy)
1 oz. (troy)	= 31.10 grains	1 gram	= .03527 oz.(avoir)
1 lb. (avoir)	= .4536 kilog.	1 kilog.	= 2.205 lb.(avoir)
1 lb. (troy)	= .3732 kilog.	1 kilog.	= 2.679 lb.(troy)
1 ton (short)	= .9072 met. ton	1 metric ton	= 1.102 tons (short)

B. FORMULAS

In the formulas given below, the following representations are used:

P	= perimeter	r	= radius
s	= side	A	= area
l	= length	b	= base
w	= width	h	= altitude
C	= circumference	V	= volume
	= 3 1/7 or 3.14 (approx.)	e	= edge
d	= diameter		

AREAS

Rectangle: $A = lw$

Parallelogram: $A = bh$

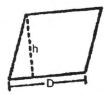

Square: $A = s^2$

Triangle: $A - 1/2\, bh$

Trapezoid: $A = 1/2h\,(b_1 + b_2)$

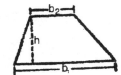

Circle: $A = \pi r^2$
Sphere: $A = 4\pi r^2$

VOLUMES

Rectangular solide (prism): $V = lwh$

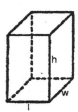

Cube: $V = e^3$

Cylinder: V - π ^{2}h

Cone: V- 1/3 π r^{2}h
Sphere: V = 4/3 π r^3

PERIMETERS

Triangle: P = s$_1$ + s$_2$ + s$_3$

Equilateral triangle: P = 3s

Square: P = 4s

Hexagon: P = 6s

Rectangle: P = 2l + 2w

Circle: C = 2π r or πd